DIVING ESCAPADES
in THAILAND'S TROPICAL SEAS

Your Underwater Guide

Sam Fang

SNP Publishers Pte Ltd

P9-AER-470

Published by
SNP Publishers Pte Ltd
97 Ubi Ave 4
Singapore 1440
Tel: 7412500
Fax: 7443770

Published 1993
All information is correct at the time of printing

Warning & Request
As time goes by, nothing stays the same. Prices may rise, schedules may change,
places may close down or open up, good places may turn bad and bad places turn
better. If you find such changes, please do not hesitate to tell us or write to us to
help update our future editions and where possible, vital changes will be included
as a STOP PRESS section in reprints. Your information will be much appreciated
and the relevant letters will receive a free copy of our Travel Guide Series.

ISBN 981-00-3825-9

Underwater Photography: Michael Lim (unless otherwise stated)
Photography: Sam Fang
Project Co-ordinator: Lyn Ee (Text, Field & Photography)

Cover: Kaleidoscopic marine colours of the Similans

Printed by Singapore National Printers Ltd

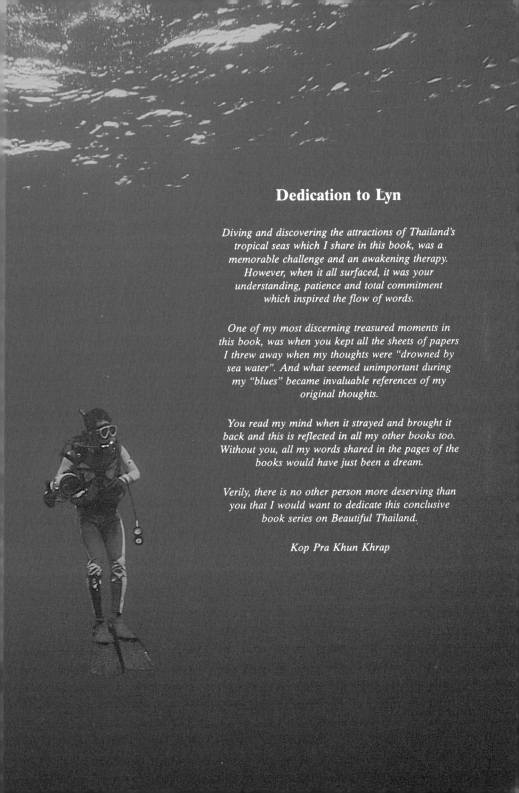

Dedication to Lyn

Diving and discovering the attractions of Thailand's tropical seas which I share in this book, was a memorable challenge and an awakening therapy. However, when it all surfaced, it was your understanding, patience and total commitment which inspired the flow of words.

One of my most discerning treasured moments in this book, was when you kept all the sheets of papers I threw away when my thoughts were "drowned by sea water". And what seemed unimportant during my "blues" became invaluable references of my original thoughts.

You read my mind when it strayed and brought it back and this is reflected in all my other books too. Without you, all my words shared in the pages of the books would have just been a dream.

Verily, there is no other person more deserving than you that I would want to dedicate this conclusive book series on Beautiful Thailand.

Kop Pra Khun Khrap

Roosting seabirds "White Capped" the rocky mount of Shark Point.

FOREWORD

It gives me great pleasure to introduce to all divers this latest addition to the growing numbers of divers' guides available in Thailand. The enthusiastic interest in Thailand's extensive coastal waters on both sides of the southern panhandle bears testimony to the country's reputation and potential as a world-class diving paradise.

As a recognition of this significant aspect of the country's tourism industry, the Tourism Authority of Thailand (TAT) has in its latest policy statement placed new emphasis on the conservation of underwater resources for tourism and the promotion of Thailand as an international haven for sports lovers. And diving is among such foremost sports of the country. As the contents of *Diving Escapades in Thailand's Tropical Seas* will make it clear to its readers, divers have an enormous variety of diving sites to choose from to suit their preferences and skills. Indeed Thailand boasts of some of the world's most majestic underwater seascapes.

This publication is in line with TAT's objectives and operations on national tourism resources and will undoubtedly assist overseas and local divers in discovering and exploring the numerous dive sites of Thailand. I would like to thank the author, his team and the publisher of the book for their dedication and contribution for promoting diving in Thailand.

DHARMNOON PRACHUABMOH
Governor — Tourism Authority of Thailand

This book — *Diving Escapades in Thailand's Tropical Seas* will delight diving enthusiasts everywhere. It has long been our wish at the TAT Diving Club to see that the spreading of information on diving sites of Thailand is promoted to as wide an audience as possible so that all lovers of the sport and the general public are made aware of the beauty of the underwater treasure of Thailand and the need for its conservation for the present and future generations.

Sam Fang came to discuss various diving issues with us some time ago. He expressed a deep understanding of the importance of the *conservation* aspect of diving sport and has keen interest in promoting diving for tourism in Thailand. For the sport to thrive and benefit the public and the tourism industry, the dual aspects of conservation and promotion must be made to complement each other, which in turn depend on the cooperation of all individuals and groups in joining in the responsible promotion and public education campaigns.

On behalf of all diving enthusiasts I would like to thank the author and his team for their efforts in introducing diving in Thailand to the international audience. We hope that Sam will continue to work on the project to update future editions and make the publication an indispensable guide for all divers.

SANTI CHUDINTRA
President: TAT Diving Club

Rare ghost pipefish, a master of camouflage.

The Author

When Sam Fang, a freelance Singaporean travel photo journalist first set foot in Thailand eleven years ago, it was the sea and the forest which captured him to stay on. Expressing his appreciation for nature's bests, he has keyed out many stories which leading travel magazines, airline inflight magazines and newspapers have published. Accredited to his involvement in promoting Thailand's diverse attractions are currently four book titles: **Bangkok's Chatuchak Weekend Market, Travel Guide – Thailand, Popular Beach Resorts – Thailand and Phuket – Jewel of the South.**

As an adventurous skin diver and scuba diver, his expressions for the treasures of the living sea, in the *Andaman Sea* and the *Gulf of Thailand*, are introduced in layman's language for the majority to enjoy this book. Sam Fang takes you on a personal tour to all the dive destinations through the turn of the pages, bringing to you the moods of dive shops, dive boats, dive sites and some close-up views of creatures in the underwater realm, based on his personal encounters.

U/W Photographer

Michael Lim, a Master Scuba Instructor is also an ardent underwater photographer for the love of the living sea. He took his first plunge in scuba diving in 1984 and has been promoting this sport ever since. He trains dive instructors, sharing with them his diving experiences in Australia, Indonesia, Malaysia, Borneo and Thailand.

Accredited to him are the establishments of 3 dive shops in Singapore, Malaysia and Thailand under the names of: **Sharkeys Dive & Adventure Singapore, Sharkeys (The Scuba Shop) Malaysia and Sharkeys Dive Shop Phuket, Thailand.**

Michael's underwater photographs reflect the spectacles of colours and characteristics of marine life and divers in action, to enhance a greater understanding of this book.

A lion fish awaits its prey.

Author's Acknowledgement

The initial raw facts of all my dives and travels to dive destinations and sites could not have been completed, if it had not been for the kind cooperation, time and knowledge of the diving fraternity, friends and organizations.

My heartfelt thanks to **Lyn Ee,** my project coordinator who stuck by me through *"stormy weather"* to refine the turn of each page and **Michael Lim** for all those beautiful marine photographs, assistance and advice when needed most. The Tourism Authority of Thailand, especially the TAT Diving Club **Santi Chudintra** who introduced me to **Sunthorn Siengsuwan,** President of the Pern Dam Nam Diving Club who in turn put me in touch with **Akom Viroj,** head of the Pattaya Sea Rescue Unit who assisted me greatly in wreck diving off Pattaya. This chain introduction was a great moral support. **Dr. Suriya** of the Underwater and Aviation Medicine Department for the invaluable information on Hyperbaric Chamber facilities. Paradise Diver of Pattaya, **Siggi, Bobby** and **Sam:** Pattaya Scuba Club, **Wolfgang:** Sharkeys Dive Shop Phuket, **Michael Lim** and **Nicholas Stoffel:** Fantasea Divers, **Jeroen C. Deknatel, Maarten N. Brusselers, Mark Stickland** and **Suzanne Forman,** Koh Samui Divers, **Cesare, Michael, Tik, Kevin** and **Mick** thanks for your intimate knowledge of Sail Rock and additional briefing of dive sites: Chumphon Cabana Dive Centre, Instructor **Sanan:** Sea and Oil Services Co Ltd, Scuba Professional **David R. Roll:** Phuket Wetsuits, **Dave** and **Pat:** Sea Bees Submarine Diving Club, **Frank:** Andaman Divers, **Prasong:** Siam Diving Centre, **John and Matthew:** Songserm Travel Center, **Thitiphong Songtrakul** and **Chanchai Songtrakul.** And **Thara Patong Beach Resort** Phuket, **Jansom Chumporn Hotel, Chaweng Regent** Koh Samui and **Wiang Thong Hotel** Krabi. **Thai Airways International** and I-Mex Travel **Phinit Chuenphimonchankit** for his invaluable computer knowledge and assistance.

And to the many other divers, boatmen, friends and King Neptune's *"disciples"* — a big thank you. Your encouragement, advice, hearty handshakes, or a mere encounter made all the difference.

Symbolic rock of Similan Island No. 8 at dawn introduces an awakening dive when marine creatures face the start of a new day.

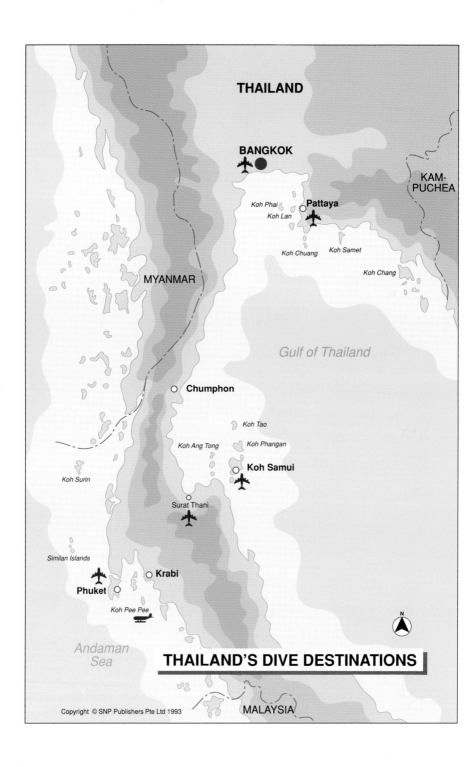

THAILAND

BANGKOK

KAM-
PUCHEA

Koh Phai
Koh Lan

Pattaya

Koh Chuang   Koh Samet

Koh Chang

MYANMAR

Gulf of Thailand

Chumphon

Koh Tao

Koh Ang Tong   Koh Phangan

Koh Surin

Koh Samui

Surat Thani

Similan Islands

Krabi

Phuket

Koh Pee Pee

N

Andaman
Sea

THAILAND'S DIVE DESTINATIONS

MALAYSIA

CONTENTS

GULF OF THAILAND

GETTING TO KNOW YOUR DIVE PROGRAMS

DIVE SITES OF KOH SAMUI

A CHIT-CHAT ON MARINE LIFE

INFORMATION

Finning towards a passing school of fish.

A compact rainbow colours of corals, fish and blue waters

INTRODUCTION

THAILAND THE VERITABLE DIVING PARADISE

Thailand's premier dive locations are comparable to some of the world class dive destinations. Its extensive coastlines fringe the *Andaman Sea* to the west between Myanmar and Peninsular Malaysia and the *Gulf of Thailand* between Kampuchea and Peninsular Malaysia to the east. There are hundreds of islands and rock outcrops where pioneering divers have charted as good dive sites and marked them on dive maps for the benefit of the diving industry and visiting divers.

A year round diving pleasure is the norm in Thailand, as both seas share alternate good season. When the south-west monsoon blows over the *Andaman Sea,* the *Gulf of Thailand* enjoys sunshine, blue skies and calm waters and vice versa, when the north-east monsoon affects the Gulf of Thailand. Hence, there will always be a favourable dive destination at any chosen time when you visit Thailand.

Thailand's tropical climate keeps the sea relatively warm and this factor, initiates one of the first comforts of diving. Its myriad seabed configurations of cliff dives, caves, steep drop-offs, "chimney" wrecks, grottos and the vast expanse of exotic coral gardens, encompass the adventure and mysteries of diving. These underwater architectures are the natural habitat to a world of exotic marine creatures which divers wish to be acquainted with. Thailand's seas are plankton rich, attracting the awe inspiring whale sharks, manta rays and a host of other pelagic fish. These marine fantasies coupled with good visibility will delight underwater photographers and marine naturalists.

The *Andaman Sea* dive destinations offer a pure diving pleasure and live aboard dive expeditions to renowned premier dive sites in the *Similan Islands, Surin Islands* and the *Burma Banks.* From Phuket, there are equally exciting daily trips to popular dive sites of *Pee Pee Islands, Racha Islands, Shark Point, Dok Mai* and west coast dive sites. Dive programs come in variety and there is always one to suit your ultimate desire.

In the *Gulf of Thailand,* **Pattaya** the *main* dive base of the eastern seaboard is also the take-off point to budding dive sites of *Koh Chang National Marine Park,* which is near the Kampuchean border. **Wreck** diving is popular in Pattaya besides dive sites off the inner and outer islands. **Chumphon** and **Koh**

1

Samui offer excellent dive sites with adventurous dives through caves, gorges, "chimneys" and a maze of pinnacles. Fish life in the surrounding waters is prolific and amassed by shoals of plankton feeders, the sightings of whale sharks and manta rays are on the records.

From Chumphon, other reputable dive sites are *Hin Lak Ngam, Koh Ngam Noi, Koh Ngam Yai* and *Hin Pae*. Those of Koh Samui reach out to the *Ang Thong National Marine Park*, rock outcrop of *Hin Bai, Koh Phangan* and *Koh Tao*.

As always mentioned, the efficient network of air, land and sea transfers to all the popular dive locations and dive sites has earned Thailand as one of the most popular diving holiday destinations by globe trotting divers. And when all your diving desires are fulfilled, you will be equally pleased with the myriad choice of optional bonanza tours, watersports, a feast of exotic local cuisines, a host of evening entertainment, great shopping and a wide range of fine accommodation to assure you a **complete** holiday.

Barrel shaped green tunicate stands out in this underwater corsage of coralline algae and brittle corals.

DIVE LINKS

Some of the reasons why Thailand is chosen as a veritable paradise in scuba diving are for its good air-links by the national carrier **Thai Airways International,** domestic flights to and from dive destinations and the joy of being able to dive two seas; the **Andaman Sea** and the **Gulf of Thailand** on a single holiday.

Bangkok and **Phuket** are international gateways to Thailand's diving holiday. And its domestic overland connections by trains and comfortable air-conditioned buses via excellent highways to the other dive destinations are efficient. Island dive destinations are linked by ferry and express boats and some by air services.

PHUKET

By Air
The popular beach resort of Phuket lies on the west side of the Kra Isthmus. *Phuket International Airport* is fast becoming a holiday stopover from neighbouring countries like Singapore, Hong Kong, Taipei, Tokyo including Penang, Langkawi and Kuala Lumpur in Peninsular Malaysia. During the peak season, the island experiences an influx of chartered flights from European countries like Amsterdam, Copenhagen, Frankfurt, London, Milan, Munich, Vienna and Zurich.

Phuket is the main take-off to diving escapades in the Andaman Sea. The island is receiving more international divers via Bangkok. **Thai Airways International** operates more than 10 daily flights to Phuket from Bangkok. During the peak and festive seasons, there are additional flights, in the week. The daily flight from **Surat Thani** offers an alternate air-route to Phuket if you miss the direct flight from the dive hub of **Koh Samui** by Bangkok Airways.

By Road
There are more than a dozen air-conditioned buses of variable classes leaving for Phuket every evening from *Bangkok* between 6.00 p.m. to 7.00 p.m. from the Southern Bus Station locally known as *Sai Tai.* This journey takes about 14 hours over 880 km.

From *Chumphon* by air-conditioned mini coach, it takes 6 hours over 470 km to reach Phuket, leaving daily at noon time. Contact local travel agencies for this service.

From *Koh Samui,* air-conditioned buses and mini coach leave the island at 7.00 a.m. via ferry service to Surat Thani on the mainland, arriving Phuket at 3.00 p.m.

PATTAYA

By Air

Currently the *U-Tapao Airport* services occasional chartered flights from Asian and European countries.

By Road

From **Bangkok** there is an air-conditioned bus leaving every 30 minutes from 6.00 a.m. to 10.00 p.m. from *Ekamai Eastern Bus Station.* This journey of 154 km takes about 3 to 4 hours, depending on the traffic situation. From *Bangkok's Don Muang International Airport* there are air-conditioned buses leaving for Pattaya at 9.00 a.m., 12 noon and 7.00 p.m.

From *Phuket* more than a dozen air-conditioned buses of variable classes leave for Bangkok daily between 3.00 p.m. and 4.00 p.m. from the *Bor-Kor-Sor* or Bus Station in town. The 14 hours journey over 880 km gets you into Bangkok in the early morning where you can have an early start to Pattaya from *Ekamai Eastern Bus Station.*

KOH SAMUI

By Air

Bangkok Airways operates 7 flights daily to Koh Samui from **Bangkok** and 2 daily flights from **Phuket.** This has great influence over the diving industry to connect the Gulf of Thailand and the Andaman Sea, linking 2 popular dive destinations. However, there is an indirect alternative route by air daily from Bangkok and Phuket to Surat Thani via a connecting ferry service to Koh Samui.

By Road/Rail

Getting to Koh Samui by road or rail, stop at Surat Thani for connecting ferry services. Air-conditioned buses to Surat Thani from Bangkok depart between 8.00 p.m. to 8.40 p.m. from the Southern Bus Station or *Sai Tai.* The journey takes approximately 10 hours over 668 km.

You may also take a train from Bangkok's *Hualamphong Railway Station.* There are 7 trains leaving daily, but the most suitable is the 6.30 p.m. train which gets you to **Surat Thani** in the early morning. There are special train service tickets that include transfers to the pier and the ferry ride to **Koh Samui.**

Visiting the popular beach resort of Koh Samui is easy from Phuket. There is a daily air-conditioned bus which leaves Phuket at 10.00 a.m. via ferry services from Surat Thani and arriving Koh Samui at 6.00 p.m. There are also air-conditioned mini coaches which can pick you up from your hotel at 8.00 a.m. arriving on Koh Samui at 4.00 p.m. The departure times for these two road transfers coincide with the commercial ferry departure time which carries vehicles and their passengers.

By Sea

Express Boat (Songserm Travel Centre)			
Surat Thani *(Thaton)* Departure	*Koh Samui* *(Nathon)* Arrival	*Koh Samui* *(Nathon)* Departure	*Surat Thani* *(Thaton)* Arrival
8.00	10.15	7.15	9.30
14.00	16.15	14.30	16.45
Koh Samui Departure	*Koh Phangan* Arrival	*Koh Phangan* Departure	*Koh Samui* Arrival
9.30	10.15	6.15	7.00
10.30	11.15	11.30	12.15
16.30	17.15	13.00	13.45
Commercial Ferry Service			
Surat Thani *(Donsak)* Departure	*Koh Samui* *(Tong Yang)* Arrival	*Koh Samui* *(Tong Yang)* Departure	*Surat Thani* *(Donsak)* Arrival
7.30	8.40	8.00	9.10
10.00	11.10	10.00	11.10
12.00	13.10	12.00	13.10
14.00	15.10	14.00	15.10
16.00	17.10	17.00	18.10

CHUMPHON

By Road/Rail

From **Bangkok** getting to Chumphon via the south bound air-conditioned buses which leaves at 9.00 p.m. is not convenient as the arrival time is between 3.00 a.m. to 4.00 a.m. However, there are special air-conditioned coaches leaving in the morning from Bangkok at 9.00 a.m. arranged by various private tour companies. All travel agents will be able to book the tickets for you.

Another alternative is to take a train service from *Bangkok's Thon Buri Railway Station* which operates daily 6 trips to Chumphon. Please note that the arrival time is either late evening or very early morning.

From **Phuket's** bus station or *Bor-Kor-Sor,* there are regular local non-air conditioned buses to Chumphon. Travelling time is about 8 hours and the first bus leaves at 6.00 a.m. and the last bus at 6.30 p.m. Contact your travel agent for special air-conditioned mini coaches leaving Phuket at noon time for a six-and-a-half hours journey to Chumphon. (This is the latest transfer route by our local travel agent).

KRABI

By Road

The province of Krabi is an up and coming dive destination. Its neighbour-ing islands and the popular Pee Pee Islands offer great sites for diving.

5

Getting there from Phuket is best done via air-conditioned coaches which will pick you from your hotel between 6.00 a.m. to 7.00 a.m. This convenient 3-hour journey is operated by a few local travel agents.

From Bangkok there are two air-conditioned bus services leaving Bangkok at 7.00 p.m. and 8.00 p.m. for a 14-hour journey over 860 km.

Pee Pee Islands

Sea Plane Service

Currently Tropical Sea Air Co., Ltd operates an air service from **Phuket International Airport** to **Patong Beach** and the **Pee Pee Islands.** In the near future, the service will be extended to Similan Islands and Krabi. Dive operators are happy with these facilities as they can work out packages for divers who prefer quick transfers to dive destinations from abroad or Bangkok.

For more information call 327138 Phuket. Upon reaching the island, you hop onto dive boats awaiting to cruise off to the dive sites. There are two daily return flights from Phuket to Pee Pee Islands. Divers flying in from abroad can take the connecting flight from Phuket International Airport.

By Sea

From Phuket there are various travel company's operating daily transfer/tour packages to Pee Pee Island in the early morning. From Pee Pee Islands, there are daily boat transfers to Krabi mainland and vice versa.

Food is never scarce for this sweetlip.

6

ANDAMAN
SEA

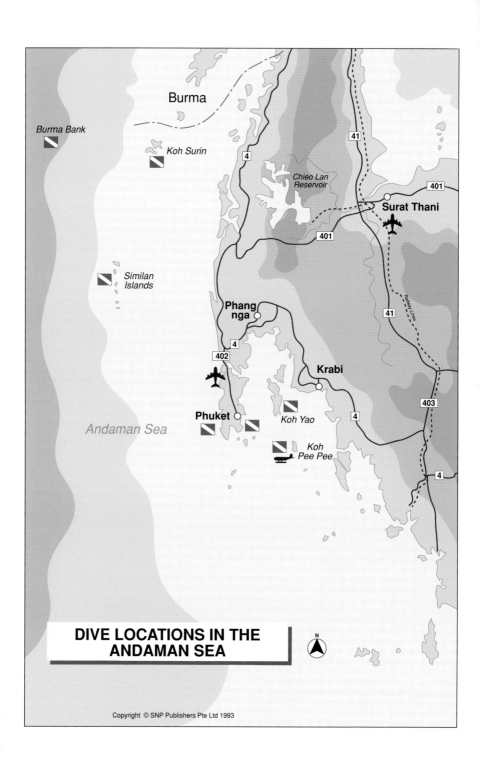

Burma

Burma Bank

Koh Surin

4

Chieo Lan
Reservoir

41

401

Surat Thani

401

Similan
Islands

Phang
nga

4

402

Krabi

41

Andaman Sea

Phuket

Koh Yao

4

403

Koh
Pee Pee

4

**DIVE LOCATIONS IN THE
ANDAMAN SEA**

N

THE ANDAMAN SEA

T he deep blues of the *Andaman Sea* surrounds hundreds of islands, islets and rocky outcrops of Thailand which border Myanmar and the north western boundary of Peninsular Malaysia. These landmarks form amazing landscapes and are surrounded by the fascinations of seascapes which are marked and charted on the maps as some of the world's best class diving sites.

Dive sites in the Andaman Sea have been acknowledged as purest diving, where coral gardens and prolific marine life are cultivated by marine phenomenon. Complementing the wealth of the sea are amazing underwater natural architecture of caves, grottos, overhanging cliffs, steep walls and shelves. These structures are habitats and playgrounds for micro-creatures to awesome *manta rays, yellow fin tunas, giant jacks, barracudas* and the *enormous whale sharks* just to name a few. Together, they fulfil a diver's dream and for these reasons, an increasing number of foreign divers now visit Phuket. And many will return yearly to explore the inexhaustible fascinations of the sea, with visibility extending to more than 35 metres.

▲ *Swim throughs at Elephant Rock in the Similan Islands provide additional thrills of diving.*

9

Premier dive sites in the Andaman Sea are located at the *Similan Islands, Surin Islands, Burma Banks, Pee Pee Islands, Racha Islands, Koh Dok Mai* and *Shark Point*. Dive expeditions to the *Similan Islands and beyond* are centred on live aboard programs while others are popular full day dive trips. There are also good dive sites surrounding the west coast of Phuket amongst myriad coves and bays. With an ample choice of dive sites to choose, a diving holiday in the Andaman Sea promises a great time.

BEST TIME TO VISIT

The best time to go diving is in November when the sea settles down after the effect of the south-west monsoon. A month delay till December is better, as the remaining floating sediments of the monsoon settles down and the visibility improves.

Good visibility holds till March and sometimes April when the sea begins its annual churn of the undercurrent to signal the entry of the south-west monsoon. After April, most foreign dive shops would have announced the close for the season.

But some dive operators conduct diving throughout the year on the eastern side of Phuket. The visibility may not be peak, however, the dive programs and sites will appease ardent divers who had overlooked the best time to visit Phuket.

Andaman Divers, a well equipped dive shop popular with visiting divers remains operational throughout the low season. Situated in the beach front road of Patong Beach amongst restaurants and hotels, walk-in customers stream in readily to admire a wall of dive related pictures and for information on where best to dive during the low season.

BLESSINGS OF THE MONSOON

Tropical monsoons bring gusty winds, torrential rain and high waves which churn the clear sea into murky waters. All tourist-related businesses and the fishing industry experience the low season "blues" during this period. Tourist traffic slackens and the prices of seafood soar as only few boats dare to venture out to the open sea.

Amidst all this gloom, monsoons are in fact, effective natural conservation factors which narrows the gap of future shortage of marine food, which is now a global concern.

Fish fry in unity.

10

During the monsoon the seabed is being churned by billowing waves, sending millions of microscopic organisms to swim in mid waters. This bounteous supply of food for the marine life population induces growth and reproduction. The south-west and north-east monsoon which last 4 and 6 months respectively prevents extensive fishing, thus, giving the marine creatures a chance to multiply and grow.

Shallower waters of coastal regions experience a greater churn from the repetitive big waves and more natural seafood surfaces in mid waters. Experiment dives during this period have revealed the influx of fish normally found in deep waters. Lobsters leave their deep lairs and are sighted under rock protuberances feeding on floating small marine animals. Crustaceans are normally nocturnal feeders.

The effect of the monsoon is an obvious blessing to marine ecology, sending "messages" to the inhabitants of the sea that it is time to feast, play and multiply with less fear of man.

Above: Sea cucumber "trunking" for food.

DIVE LOCATIONS AND SITES IN THE ANDAMAN SEA

The Andaman Sea which spans the west coast of the Kra Isthmus plays host to numerous rocky outcrops and islands which form the popular dive rendezvous for today's ardent scuba divers.

The diving industry in the Andaman Sea is complete in offering the ultimate diving pleasure. The build up was primarily started by foreign divers who were charmed by the fantasy of the seabed and the opportunity to start a diving business.

As stated, **Phuket**, is the major take-off point to all the dive locations and its surrounding waters in the west coast offers good dive sites too. Some of the world's best dive locations and sites are found in the **Andaman Sea.** Let me now introduce to you their whereabouts and characteristics with charts to follow. After reading about the individual dive locations, you may want to explore more than just one, two or three. In this case, please refer to the groupings to understand their locations for constructive planning.

DIVE LOCATIONS IN THE ANDAMAN SEA

DESTINATION	LOCATION	DIVE SITE	DEPTH	SEASCAPE & MARINE LIFE
PHUKET	West Coast	Koh Pu	10–20m	Underwater boulders & sporadic coral life and reef patch. Reef sharks & mid-water predator pelagic fish.
		Ley Hua Nawn	10–25m	Flat reef & rocky slopes. Sighting of big migratory fish.
		Off Freedom Beach	20–25m	Patch reef forming labyrinth. Strong current.
		Patong Southern Reef	5–15m	Fringing reef, reef patch & rocky seabed. Abundant aquarium fish.
		Patong Northern Reef	5–18m	Artificial reef, fringing reef, reef patch and rocky seabed. Turtle sighting.
		Kamala Rock Outcrop	10–18m	Patch reef. Rocky bottom. Pelagic fish sighting.
		Off Laem Singh Beach	8–15m	Huge mass of boulder coral forming a plateau. Abundant damsels and yellow tail fish.
	East Coast Offshore Islands	Shark Point (Hin Musang)	10–22m	Marine sanctuary, fish feeding and possible sighting of leopard sharks.
		Koh Dok Mai	22–25m	Deep wall and cave dive. Soft flower corals, bivalves and anemone.
		Koh Mai Thon	18–22m	Sporadic reef & evidence of reef destruction. Strong current and abundant sea urchins.
		Racha Islands	15–28m	Fringing reef and rocky seabed. Strong current. Steep drop and possible sighting of game fish.
		Coral Island (Koh Hae)	10–18m	Garden of hard corals and rocky seabed. Aquarium fish, horse and Indian mackerels and anemone.
	Pee Pee Islands	Maya Bay	15–20m	Patch reefs, wall and cave dive. Sail fish sighting may be possible in late afternoon.
		Loh Samah Bay	10–22m	Wall and crevice dive. Abundant flora and fauna with lots of bivalve shells attaching onto sea fan and coral.
		Bidah Islands	18–30m	Wall dives, sporadic coral patches on seabed.
		Hin Pae	10–15m	Good example of coral reef formation. Reef flat, reef crest, reef slope and patch reef.
	Krabi	Koh Mae Urai	15–18m	Irregular eroded rock with small archways and labyrinth to explore. Fish life not abundant and corals scanty.

DESTINATION	LOCATION	DIVE SITE	DEPTH	SEASCAPE & MARINE LIFE
		Koh Ya Wa Bon	8–15m	Abundant fish life and the spotting of reef shark common. There are limestone archways and grottos.
	Similan Islands	Island No.#8 (Koh Similan)	20–25m	A great community of corals and a galaxy of exotic aquarium fish welcome divers. Amazement and appreciation of the living sea prevails. Possible night diving at the edge of the bay.
		Island No. #9 (Koh Bangu)	10–15m	Adventurous diving. Caverns, swim throughs and unusual rock formations. Possible sighting of big pelagic fish.
		Elephant Rock (Hin Pousar)	15–20m	Voted as the most gorgeous dive site for new and veteran divers. It has the combination of rich marine life from corals to fish amongst huge boulders, caves and gorges.
		Island No.#4 (Koh Miang)	15–20m	Reef flat environment with gradual undulating formation. Patch reef obvious between sandy area of low mount corals. Night diving is encouraged.
		Island No.#7 (Koh Payu)	15–18m	Rocky headland tapers and continue its characteristics on the seabed. Parrot fish and yellow snappers abundant and the sighting of the reef black tip shark is often.
		Island No.#1 (Koh Huyong)	10–15m	A colourful coral garden in shallow waters. Great site for comfortable dive before the expedition ends.
	Burma Bank		15–20m	Fields of juvenile staghorn corals, more near the slopes. Pore corals, table corals are sporadic with blue coloured finger sponges and they are homes to oriental sweetlips, snappers, nurse sharks and families of smaller fish and crustaceans. Mid water fish are the dog-tooth-tunas, rainbow runners, jacks and silver breams. Triggers and moray eels are found near crevices on the slopes. The awesome silver tip sharks lurk in deeper waters at the drop-offs.
	Surin Islands	Richelieu Rock	15–30m	Great chance to sight whale sharks and manta rays. Fish traps and torn fish nets amongst rocky seabed and fringing reef. Cuttlefish mating is a possible sighting from late November to February.
		Koh Ta Chai	16–24m	Abundant soft corals, sea fan, sea whip and pore corals. Shoals of fish fry gather at coral heads and crevices. Groupers, snappers and jacks dart around and feed on these fry.

Racoon Butterfly fish in privacy.

PHUKET

The province of Phuket is the largest island in the Kingdom with a hilly terrain land mass of about 550 sq.km. The island now attracts international divers to the Andaman Sea because of its excellent locations and back-up facilities. It is the main dive base in the region and majority of the dive trips to popular destinations like *Similan Islands, Surin Islands, Burma Banks* and *Pee Pee Islands* takes off from Phuket.

Dive shops, dive boats, dive instructors and international dive associations are all on this island, to form the springboard to the Andaman Sea. There is an adequate spread of diving facilities on the island with a back up of international dive instructors and language is the least problem. Dive flags carrying the names like PADI, NAUI and SSI make it easy to become members of the scuba diving teams.

Most dive shops operated by foreigners will be closed during the off season. Local dive shops which remain operational throughout the off season conduct dive programs only to the east coast where the sea routes are not affected by the full lashes of the south-west monsoon. The Similan Islands, Surin Islands and beyond are out of bounds.

OLD PHUKET....

A "dive" into old Phuket will enhance your appreciation the path which the island took in the early years. As far back as the early 14th century, European seafaring traders saw the island, then known by so many other names as a favourable trading base. The Portuguese, Dutch and English too had an interest and gave names to the island like *Jan-sylam, Insalan, Junkceylon* to *Bhuket, Poket* and *Phuket.*

Tin-mining onshore and offshore were the main source of natural wealth of the island. The rich deposits and venturing European tin mining companies created jobs for the locals. Tin mining workers came from Peninsular Malaysia, Burma, India, China and the Sea Gypsies who were the earliest settlers. This created a multi-racial population with the majority being Chinese. Today, Chinese influence is evident in the language, foods, traditions, culture and architecture. Phuket has been considered a Thai-Chinese community in many respects.

The natural wealth of the island gave rise to four Burmese invasions, but none successful in capturing the island. The first invasion fought in 1785 was the Battle of Thalang which cited the brave leadership of two sisters, *Khunying Chan* and *Khunying Mook* who led the local defence to victory. Their monument now stands on a crossroad on the main highway from the airport.

Civil riots amongst Chinese traits started a serious island wide turmoil which was eventually quelled by *Abbot Luang Po Chaem* of Chalong Temple, who was believed to have magical powers. This temple is now popularly visited by locals and tourists alike. In the early 1900s, Phuket became a self-supporting island with brisk trading from tin, rubber and marine products. The appointment of *Governor Kho Sim Bee (Phraya Ratsada)* brought modern changes from building of the first bank, hospitals, trading markets, schools and the harbour. He is recognised as the model Governor of modern Phuket.

About two decades ago, backpackers travelled the difficult roads to the west coast where they found unsurpassed natural beauty of isolated white sandy beaches and clear waters. Swimming, snorkelling and discovering the wealth of coral reefs became the dream for early visitors. The news spread fast and more visitors came, huts and cottages were built and Patong Beach felt its first impact of foreign tourists.

The Tourism Authority of Thailand gave this rough "diamond" a polish in 1973. The island's development has had a snowballed effect ever since. Phuket entered a new era of development and has gained international recognition as a popular beach resort and dive hub of Thailand.

PHUKET TODAY....

Complementing these natural attractions today are a wide spread of fine beach resort hotels, from five star to authentic bungalows. Beach activities are highlighted by a bonanza of watersports from sailing to the thrills of jet-skis and speedboats. Seafood restaurants assure a feast of a life time, and as shopping becomes second nature on a holiday, Phuket offers variable souvenir items from Thai silk to gems and wood carvings.

Optional tours put you on island discoveries and there are currently three golf courses of international standard. The swing of entertainment from nightclubs, karaokes and discotheques are found on all the popular beaches and town.

A landscape and seascape of artistic rock sculpture — Ley Hua Nawn
(Note the resemblance of Frankenstein on this boulder and a side profile of a smiling face at the left corner).

16

GETTING TO KNOW YOUR DIVE PROGRAMS

Getting to know your dive programs can be as easy as calling your tour desk at the hotel, for established dive shops have branched out their services to hotels on popular beaches like Patong, Relax Bay, Karon and Kata beaches. Most dive shops are located along the road facing the beach and some on adjoining side roads.

Shop names and their attractive diving signs have prominent international dive flags with logos and signs varying from a man-sized geared up diver to drawings of divers riding on a manta ray or on whale sharks. The diving business and its popularity of the sport has created healthy competition for the business.

Some dive shops render underwater video filming services and you may become an instant "star" in an impromptu underwater scenario. Usually divers in groups opt for this service for an agreed fee and they eventually carry home with them *"treasures"* of marine life with themselves as vistors of *Neptune's* realm.

If you are in Phuket for a short holiday and wish to see other attractions

as well, opt for the west coast dives. This dive can be done almost immediately if you have a minimum of 2 divers. If you are a single diver, the dive shop will ask you to pay a surcharge.

▲ *Preparation for wall dive at Dok Mai dive site.*

17

The east coast offshore island dives, offer deeper waters and a richer variety of marine life. The program begins with a minimum number of four divers to warrant the charter of a dive boat. The dive package will cost about 40 percent more than the west coast dive package because the sites are located further away.

Dive expeditions offer the ultimate diving pleasure in the Andaman Sea. There are signs in front of dive shops to indicate the dates of departure. Established dive shops have fixed dive schedule dates of departure to destinations like Similans, Burma Banks, Surin and Pee Pee Islands.

ONE DAY WEST COAST DIVE

There are various sites on the west coast of Phuket which are popularly introduced by dive operators using longtail boats, and bigger dive boats are used when there is a large group of divers. It takes about 20 to 40 minutes to reach the dive sites and all these largely depend on the location and prevailing weather conditions. You can either do a morning dive from 0900 hours or an afternoon dive from 1400 hours.

The chartered longtail boat awaits on the shallow waters and all divers wade towards it and climb on board. When the dive equipment is loaded, the boat heads on to the dive site, jiving and breaking waves along the way.

As soon as the boat is tied to the buoy and anchoring is secured, you begin your first dive. The depths vary from 10 to 22 metres and your second dive commences after lunch and a rest on a selected beach nearby. After the second dive the boatman starts the engine and heads back. Normally the boatman and

dive crew carry the tanks and equipment ashore, but divers in team spirit lend a hand.

Above: The anemone tentacles cushion a clown fish at rest.

Climbing into the longtail boat requires some caution when on coming waves get a little rough on the shore. Climb in only when the wave passes and quickly before the next wave comes along. You may lose your balance when you are caught with a foot on the sand and the other in the boat when the wave tosses the boat. This precaution applies when you are getting off the boat and the practical way is to sit on the edge and get off with both feet together.

ONE DAY EAST COAST OFFSHORE ISLAND DIVE

Bigger dive boats are used on this dive program and the travelling time varies from 1½ hours to 3 hours, depending on the location.

Departure point is Chalong Bay, where most dive boats are moored. Unless of course there are some special arrangements when the dive boat meet divers off an agreed beach. In this case, the versatile longtail boat is used to transfer you to the big dive boat. At Chalong Bay, you may use the jetty if the boat comes alongside, at high tide. However, most of the time, longtail boats are used to transfer divers and their equipment to the dive boat which is moored off the jetty.

Racha Islands, Shark Point, Koh Dok Mai and *Coral Island* are four of the popular dive sites offering myriad attractions. Dive boats leave the bay between 9.00 to 10.00 a.m. and your first dive begins before noon. Fifteen minutes before reaching the site, the dive master will give a briefing and checks all equipment.

Divers may experience a different site on their second dive and this depends on the experienced dive master who knows best, if it is necessary to switch dive sites.

Coral Island provides the nearest and convenient diving escapades during the low season when monsoon waves rule the *Andaman Sea*. Only a short stretch of rough sea is experienced from the take off point at Chalong Bay. Although Pee Pee Island is the other alternative, rough open sea conditions occasionally cause boat transfers to be cancelled.

See Bees Submarine Diving Club located on the short road to Chalong Bay remains open throughout the year. They have an operational unit on Coral Island which services ardent divers and student divers who are in Phuket during this period. Its dive shop, located a few metres from the white sandy beach which tapers to surrounding coral reefs is a favourite rendezvous not only for divers, but also holiday makers. Accommodation and restaurant facilities on the island enhance dive moods throughout the seasons.

ANDAMAN SEA DIVE EXPEDITIONS

The *Andaman Sea* diving packages lasts between 5 to 7 days and takes you to the *Similan Islands, Surin Islands* and the latest dive sites at *Burma Banks*. Most dive operators are well versed and organized in the Similan's package. This is because the dive location for the last 5 years has been actively promoted.

Exploring dive sites off Surin Islands is in fact an extension of the Similan package located about 50 nautical miles north. Only a handful of operators conduct this trip. The waters of Surin Islands has not been fully explored. The *Burma Banks* are open reefs located some 40 nautical miles away from the *Surin Islands*. If you have not made your bookings from overseas to dive in the Similans through some of the well established dive operators, do not worry for there are other opportunities. The numerous dive shops on popular beaches display dates as to when they leave for Similans so that walk-in divers can sign up for the trip.

Above: Students of Sea Bees Submarine Diving Club at Coral Island.

19

Currently there are sailing yachts, wooden dive and steel boats doing these dive charters. It is the trend to leave Phuket in the evening and arrive at the designated site in the early morning. Boats leave between 8.00 to 10.00 p.m., the faster boats leave later. The open sea with all its unpredictable characteristics does not allow a fixed time of arrival, but as a guideline, it takes between 6 to 8 hours. The evening departure is excellent for divers to enjoy the starry moonlight and a rest before commencing for the first dive in the morning.

On that evening before departure, you will finally meet your diving companions. Some operators would have loaded their provisions and equipment earlier, others do it when divers are transferred to the boat in the evening. Sometimes longtail boats are used in the transfers, but most dive boats have their own dinghy.

If you are on a M-V dive boat, the upper deck is a quiet and popular place for all divers to gather for some hot drinks and snacks. When you are on a sailing yacht, the deck is the ideal place for a get-to-know-each-other session.

Excitement will keep you awake till the wee hours, however, bunks are provided for slumber. It is also common for some to sleep in the open until it gets too chilly.

When the boat reaches its site, the drop of the anchor will awaken you and you will feel the difference in the boat's motion when it is secured on a buoy. Breakfast is served at the break of light before gearing for the first dive.

On an average, you will get three dives per day and a night dive. Once you are within the clear waters to begin your discovery, there will be ample time to relax and allow the mind to wander and appreciate the values of your diving adventure. Hot meals are served with a free flow of beverages throughout the journey but on some dive packages, you may have to pay for soft drinks.

Occasional beaching gives a lovely break from seascapes to landscapes. The soft white sand on the beach is so inviting and rock structures in the Similans are simply awesome. When the crew goes ashore with their dinghy sometimes for a supply of fresh water or to bury their garbage, hitch a ride and spend some time exploring the hinterlands. It is great fun to climb some of the rocky landscapes, especially at the *Island No. #8* at the Similans.

Above: Close-up of cave coral yellow polyps.

The *Similan Islands* adventure is usually 5 to 6 days and the long trip includes diving in Surin waters and the Burma Banks which cover a 7 to 9 day program. Dive pattern differs with different dive shops and there are no fixed routes as sometimes detours are required due to weather conditions.

Some air compressors can be a distraction in the still silence of the sea.

It may disturb you, but there is ample space on board the boat to get away. This noise pollution is inevitable as it is part and parcel of this sport. You will love the sport more towards the end of the dive expedition. Time will seem to have whizzed by so fast that you would wish it was all just beginning. On the other hand, the hinterland attractions in Phuket will give you more holiday pleasure.

PHUKET'S DIVE BOATS

Above: The Sai Mai II — a 21 metre hardwood custom built dive boat of Siam Diving Center.

Phuket as a major dive base to the Andaman Sea has a fleet of variable dive boats, from the versatile longtail boats which are popularly used for neighbouring dive sites to sophisticated sailing yachts, wooden and steel hull vessels. As competition in the diving industry builds up, boat owners upgrade their facilities to pamper discerning globe trotting divers.

An Experience With The Longtail Boat

The name given to this type of boat is on account of its long propeller shaft driven by an engine. Longtail boats are wooden boats measuring about 8-9 metres, tapered at both ends, with the broadest point at mid-section measuring about 2 metres wide. The draft is about a half metre and it has a high prow. Its broad mid section, high prow, low draft and tapered ends make a longtail very versatile and stable in shallow waters or on a rough sea.

A longtail boat serves well on dive sites located near tricky rock outcrops when anchorage is very near to overhanging cliffs. This boat can accommodate six divers and a dive master comfortably.

Longtail boats are commonly used when diving on the west coast. This program includes two dives with an interval ashore for a light snack at the nearest selected beach. The break coincides with the safe surface interval time and of course a chance to visit a different beach.

On board the longtail boat, dive operators would have had all tanks, regulators and buoyancy compensators rigged up as movement is limited. This enables divers to put on the mask, fins and weight belt and be ready for a reverse roll over method into the waters at the shortest time. For your second dive, the experienced boatman and dive master will change the air tanks before you get on board the boat.

A sense of balance is required and cooperation amongst divers is essential. Although the boat is stable, it naturally keels when more weight is on one side. Hence, it is good to have two divers on each side of the boat taking off at the same time. Some longtail boats have short ladders, others may not have. Those without ladders may impose some difficulty for divers who are heavy and not physically trim when they are trying to get on the boat after the dive. Request for a longtail boat with ladders if possible.

Above: Songserm Sea King II ferry divers and non divers to the Similans from Patong Beach.

Above: Versatile longtail boats are used for west coast dives (Phuket).

When There Is No Ladder
Approach the boat, remove weight belt, tanks and BC and have the boatman haul it up. Pull down the mask and move it behind the head so that it will not hamper your ascend. Keep the fins on as

it will assist you in the upward thrust movement when you are using your arms as leverage to get on the boat. Failing to get onto the boat in this manner, the boat will be keeled to decrease the draft to enable you to climb aboard.

Sometimes these two methods may fail and continuous attempts will lead to exhaustion. In this case, the dive master or your partner can assist by first jumping into the water with his mask and fins on; takes a deep breath and submerges his head and shoulders while holding on to the edge of the boat with both hands. You then remove your fins and climb on his shoulder to get on the boat. This method is used as a last resort. Buoyancy in water helps reduce weight, thus the strain on the "human ladder" is less.

If you have not experienced diving from a longtail boat, it is an adventure, but when the sea is choppy, your balancing act, will be an added story to tell.

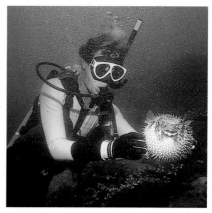

Above: Not encouraged, but divers do get carried away with this puffer fish affair.

Wooden Vessel Dive Boats

Some Thai fishing boats have been converted into dive boats, and there are also custom-built wooden hull dive boats too. Some boats undergo moderate changes, but others have undergone extensive additional fixtures to suit top class diving. A few of those wooden vessels are upgraded to standard, acceptable by international marine insurance companies and certified for ocean travelling.

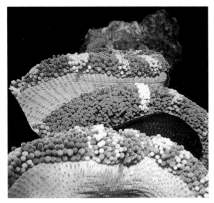

Above: A damsel "cushions" itself amidst the folds of anemones.

Most of these bigger and better equipped dive boats are owned by foreigners who understand the detail requirements for international divers to have an enjoyable diving holiday. Besides a good menu aboard, the trend is shifting towards air-conditioned cabins, video rooms and a library too.

These boats cater for a different class of divers who have the budget to enjoy the extra facilities, but there are also good dive boats to suit all divers' budget.

Most boats have an upper deck for divers to relax and to be away from engine and compressors' noise. But if you are prone to motion sickness, it is best to stay at the lower deck.

One of the most practical and popular features is a suitable dive platform at the stern. Those with tank slots and benches make diving a whole lot more comfortable. Divers need not have to congest on the deck while gearing or taking-off dive equipment.

The *Sai Mai II*, a custom built dive boat of *Siam Diving Center* in its class, exemplifies a classic live-aboard vessel which is designed by divers for divers. This 21-metre dive boat accommodates only 8 guest divers in its four air-conditioned double occupancy cabins. And that leaves ample space for divers to enjoy its sun deck, salon, spacious dive platform, hot showers and other dive related facilities.

Dive and Sail

Cruising on a sailing yacht to your dive destination captures a double pleasure of diving and sailing.

Phuket is the favourite rendezvous for 50 to 60 sailing yachts during the high season. Some are visitors from distant land on a holiday, others come yearly to charter their yachts to dive companies, while others are resident sailing yachts.

Those which are rigged for dive charters are equipped with facilities from compressors, tank holders to dive platform. Captains regard their sailing yachts as "homes" at sea, hence divers experience personalized services in the comforts of variable interior designs. Facilities on board may include desalination machines, micro-ovens and other modern gadgets. The interior of cabins and main salon give a personal touch and together, all these may cost divers more but it's worth the extra luxury.

Sailing yachts usually moor in sheltered waters and some utilize their robust inflatable dinghies with outboards to transfer divers with full gears on to neighbouring dive sites. Dinghy renders great stability. However, if divers are gearing up in the dinghy, the space is limited and the body movements may need adjustments like having to kneel or turn around in a squatting manner when gearing up. The hang of it will come quite naturally for you to adapt to the situation with the dive master at hand to assist.

Low draft of the dinghy enables you to get into the water easily with a side or back roll. Getting into the dinghy after you have taken off your gears is not difficult either. Just in case for some reason you are unable to climb in, go to the stern and step on the ledge near the engine propeller or sometimes there are rear tow rings to assist as steps. This operation is well conducted and you are ensured of minimum strain. After your dive, just climb on board the yacht and let the crew take care of the rest.

Dinghy operation is conducted more often when the sailing yacht is moored in calm waters and the dive sites are away from the lee. This method is very much favoured, as divers after dives can rest in the comfort of calm waters. (Other dive boats with dinghies, conduct this style of diving when the situation warrants)

Fast Boat Transfers

When time is not in your hands and yet, your urge to dive at Pee Pee Islands or even the Similan Islands is great; turn to fast boat transfers and enjoy the fantasies of the deep.

Available currently are a fleet of variable deep V-hull imported speed-boats powered by twin 200 h.p. to whisk divers to distant dive locations at top speed and less time.

Operators of these fast speedboats are either catering for transfers alone and work in close link with dive shops, or they are a division of the dive shop.

With the travel time cut down, divers are assured of at least two dives at distant dive locations. The exact number of tanks and dive equipment are ferried along with refreshments and food aboard on these fast boat dive expeditions.

Songserm Travel Center's fast boat, the **Sea King II** which is capable of ferrying 250 passengers in 3 hours to the Similan Islands, has paved the way for more visitors and divers to visit the scenic archipelago. For those who wish to have the comforts of air-conditioning, there are 58 seats available. They operate on Tuesday and Saturday, leaving Patong Beach at 8.00 a.m. and returning by 6.30 p.m. The first stop will be Island No. #4 and the second stop, Island No. #8.

Divers keen to dive in the Similans and be back on the same day can make arrangements with the dive shop. They can enjoy the services on board the fast boat which includes fruits, snacks, beverages and lunch. Non-divers explore the beaches, swim and snorkel amongst gin clear waters or hike up the symbolic rock at Island No. #8.

Steel Hull Dive Boats

The era of steel hull dive boats to join the fleet in Phuket is here. After **Fantasea Divers Co Ltd** acquired the 30 metre **M.V. Fantasea**, a 110 ton steel hull vessel built in Germany had it completely refitted from the keel up in 1990.

Powered by twin 700 h.p. diesel engines and a fuel capacity capable of conducting a 60 hours cruising speed at 15 knots, it is one of the dive boats which can perform a return journey to the Burma Banks which covers approximately 700 kilometres.

Some of the features on board are: carpeted air-conditioned cabins, bathrooms with hot showers, battery charging facilities of 220 volts, a video room and an E-6 film processing facility. The vessel can accommodate 18 divers and 8 crew members.

Additional boats of this capacity and more, will escalate new discovery dive sites for the diving industry in Phuket.

Above: Personalised underwater video services available on popular dive destinations.

Above: A pair of three banded butterfly fish "romancing" above a gathering of feather star.

25

DIVE PACKAGES FROM PHUKET

Prices in dive packages may vary according to the program, the duration, the type of dive boats and its facilities on board from accommodation, to the quality of meals served in the case of dive expeditions, As a general guideline:

One Day West Coast Dive ....800–1,200 baht
(2 dives inclusive of tanks & weight belt only)
Operators..All dive shops

One Day East Coast Offshore Island Dive:
Coral Island ....1,000–1,200 baht
(2 dives inclusive of tanks & weight belt only)
Racha Islands ....1,400–1,600 baht
(2 dives inclusive of tanks & weight belt only)
Dok Mai/Shark Point ....1,400–1,800 baht
(2 dives inclusive of tanks & weight belt only)
Operators ....All dive shops

One Day Pee Pee Island Dive ....2,000–2,200 baht
(2 dives inclusive of tanks & weight belt only)
2 Days 1 Night Pee Pee Island Dive ....4,800–5,000 baht
(4 dives, inclusive of accommodation on Pee Pee Don, full equipment)
Operators ....All dive shops

Andaman Sea Dive Expedition:
Similan Islands (5 to 6 days) ....12,000–15,000 baht
(unlimited dives, live aboard, full equipment)
Operators ....All dive shops

Similans/Surin/Burma Banks ....25,000–37,000 baht
(US$1,000–US$1,500)
(unlimited dives, live aboard, full equipment)
Current Operators ....Fantasea Divers/S.E.A. Yacht Charter/Siam Diving Center

PHUKET'S DIVING FRATERNITY

Andaman Divers
83 Moo 3 Thaveewong Road
(KSR Bungalow) Patong Beach
Phuket 83150
Tel/Fax: (076) 341126
Hot Line: 01-9564080
Local dive operator

Fantasea Divers
93/58 Moo 4 Thaveewong Road
Patong Beach, Phuket 83150
Tel: (076) 340088
Fax: (076) 340309
5 Star Diving Courses

Siam Diving Center
121/9 Patak Road, Mu 4
Kata/Karon Beach
Phuket 83100
Tel: (076) 330936
Tel/Fax: (076) 330608
5 Star Instructor Development Center

Sea Bees Submarine Divine Club
1/3 Viset Road
Ao Chalong, Phuket 83130
Hotline: 01 7230893
Tel/Fax: (076) 381765
Only a sprint to the hub of dive boats

P.I.D.C. Divers
1/10 Viset Road
Chalong Bay, Phuket 83130
Tel & Fax: (076) 381219
A touch of foreign & local dive moods

Sharkeys Dive Shop
47/48 Moo 3 Soi Nam Yen,
Sawadirak Road
Patong Beach, Phuket 83150
Tel/Fax: (076) 341595, 340457,
Cosmopolitan dive moods

Barakuda Diving Centre
Patong Beach, Phuket

Ocean Divers
83/59 Moo 3 Thaveewong Road
Patong Beach, Phuket 83150
Tel: (076) 341273, Fax: (076) 341274
Tel/Fax: (076) 340625
Local dive operator

Marina Divers
P.O. Box 143, Phuket 83000
Kata/Karon Beach,
Tel: (076) 330625, 330517
Fax: (076) 330516
A friend of King Neptune's realm

Kon-Tiki Diving School
66/3-65/1 Patak Road
Karon Beach, Phuket 83100
Tel: (076) 330048
Tel/Fax: (076) 330468
Swedish 5 Star I.D.C. Center

Neptun Diving
92/23 Sawasdirag Road,
Patong Beach, Phuket 83150
Tel: (076) 340585
Informal services

Santana Diving Centre
P.O. Box 79 Phuket 83000
Patong Beach Tel/Fax: (076) 340360
Kata/Karon Tel/Fax: (076) 330598
Seascape & Landscape Adventure

Holiday Diving Club
P.O. Box 27, Patong Beach
Phuket 83150
Tel: (076)341235, Fax: (076) 340998

Phuket Aquatic Safari
62/9 Rasada Road, Phuket 83000
Tel: (076) 216562, Fax: (076) 214507

S.E.A. Yacht Charter
Patong Beach, Phuket

H20 Sportz
Pansea Hotel, Phuket

Scuba World
Patong Beach, Phuket

Transparent Beauty.

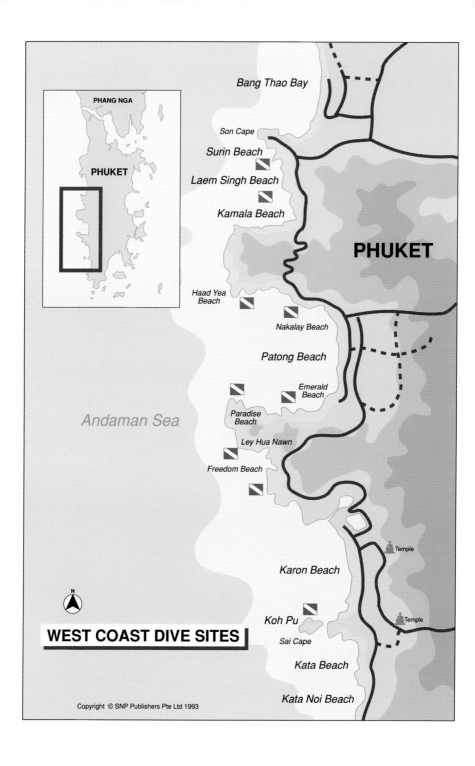

PHANG NGA

PHUKET

Bang Thao Bay

Son Cape

Surin Beach

Laem Singh Beach

Kamala Beach

PHUKET

Haad Yea
Beach

Nakalay Beach

Patong Beach

Andaman Sea

Emerald
Beach

Paradise
Beach

Ley Hua Nawn

Freedom Beach

Temple

Karon Beach

N

Koh Pu

Sai Cape

Temple

WEST COAST DIVE SITES

Kata Beach

Copyright © SNP Publishers Pte Ltd 1993

Kata Noi Beach

WEST COAST DIVE SITES
OF PHUKET

A combination of differing seabed formations from coral reefs to rocky boulders and a wealth of marine life at west coast dive sites are within easy reach and require minimum preparation. Dive shops are adequate, longtail boats easily available and together with a host of programs introduce the popular one day pleasure diving.

Access

All the dive sites on the west coast are approachable from any of the beaches. Longtail boats are commonly used when there are 2 to 6 divers on the trip. A big dive boat is chartered only for a group of 8 to 12 divers on the same trip.

KOH PU

Dive sites surrounding this uninhabited islet are nearest from Kata and Karon beaches. Dive shops promote frequent dive trips from these two beaches for its close proximity and easy access.

Characteristics

Underwater boulders, sporadic coral life and reef patches. Reef sharks and mid-water predator pelagic fish. Dive depth: 10–20 metres.

Dive Scenes

Doing a reconnoitre dive around this small island gives you an understanding of the changing characteristics of the seabed. The undulating depth varies, with corals and marine life abundant amongst piles of rocks and boulders. Holes and small caves amongst the pile-ups are natural habitat to fishes like snappers, sweetlips and groupers which will curiously play hide-and-seek with you as you descend. You may occasionally see big pelagic fish like jacks, queenfish and barracudas in shoals darting close to the rocks feeding on fish fry. Commonly seen are some territorial reef sharks which usually keep their distance. They lurk around the north western side where rocky seabed tapers to deep sandy open waters.

There is a patch of coral reef in a channel between Koh Pu and the shores of Karon and Kata beaches. In this channel, the current can be very strong on the residing tide. The reef patches extend sporadically towards Kata Beach and stop short where it is sandy.

Time break before the second dive on this program is either on the quiet corners of Kata or Karon Beach. A short drift diving can be interesting on

▲ *Koh Pu only a few metres from Karon and Kata beaches where breaking waves encourage body surfing.*

this channel for the second dive when strong current prevails. Chances of sighting big pelagic fish are good when the current is strong.

LEY HUA NAWN BAY & OFF FREEDOM BEACH

These two sites south of Patong Beach before Relax Beach are described together as they are located close to each other and either sites are chosen for the first and second dive.

Characteristics

Ley Hua Nawn — A flat reef containing a variety of coral/rocky slopes and undulating boulder formation. Possible sightings of big migratory fish during peak tides or on a sunny day, and black

tip reef sharks add to the families of fish. Dive depth : 10 – 25 metres.

Dive Scenes

The whole bay of *Ley Hua Nawn* is practically covered with different species of corals. Divers constant companion are the parrot fish, surgeon, rabbit and stripe-tank fish which swim around as you descend. Small schools of green damsels often follow the rising air bubbles as you make your way within the bay area for a closer observation of smaller marine creatures hidden amongst the crevices of brain and boulder corals. Rainbow-runners, barracudas, queenfish and jacks are often seen in the early afternoon during peak tide at the northern tip of the bay. Here, crevices and cave-ins amongst the boulders are homes to lobsters, snappers, groupers, sting-rays and other non-migratory fish. The black tip reef sharks here are well fed and usually appear for a curious look. The crown-of-thorn starfish, predator of coral reefs are abundant at this dive site.

Characteristics

Off Freedom Beach — Patch reef in rows forming a labyrinth. Strong current prevails. Dive depth: 20 – 25 metres.

Dive Scenes

Off Freedom Beach dive site lies approximately 300 metres from the centre of the beach. Coral encrusted rocks here form an underwater labyrinth adjoining each other at different levels. This undulating patch reef in the path of strong currents attract divers. But sometimes, the effect of the current may cause some divers to feel disoriented. At this site it is advisable to follow the dive master and not stray away on your own. There is a lack of rich coral formation on these maze of rocks as they are within the path of strong currents. Families of coral fish are not dense, however, colonies of red coral trouts with blue spots are abundant here and are seen peering from coral heads curiously. The small species of yellow tail snappers are abundantly swimming in mid-waters feeding on plankton. Looking upwards on the ascend, you may see shoals of garfish in hot pursuit for small fish. In a dash of speed after its prey or in fright, garfish can reel on the surface of the sea on its tail for quite a distance. This feat has often amazed many visitors viewing from the boat.

Freedom Beach is the favourite rendezvous for rest time in between dives. Here the soft talcum white sand, clear waters, elegant coconut palms and shady cashew trees extend their welcome. There is no accommodation on this unspoilt beach, except for a quaint restaurant which serves food and drinks to visitors. Its unclustered natural atmosphere here attracts many tourists from Patong Beach by longtail boats.

PATONG BAY (SOUTHERN REEF AND NORTHERN REEF)

Popular *Patong Beach* has excellent closeby dive sites within its bay. Awaiting to be discovered are healthy reefs which virtually start a few metres from the corners of the beach, extending to the entrance of the bay. These natural gifts to divers are found in greater numbers with dense reefs off isolated small beaches and coves found along the curves of the bay. Dive trips here are made via longtail boats which approach the isolated beaches during break time and before the second dive.

Characteristics

Patong Northern and Southern reefs — Families of corals abound with a wide variety of aquarium fish life. A depth of 5 to 18 metres average around the bay. The reef formation expands from 20 to 50 metres wide before sliding into a seabed of sand and isolated patches of small rocks. This general pattern can be noticed clearer when you are on top of cliffs looking down on the bay. The clear waters comes in two colours, the darker blue reflects seabed of coral reefs and emerald green indicates sandy seabed.

Dive Scenes

The *southern reefs* off Emerald Beach and its connecting Paradise Beach near the entrance of Patong Bay have similar coral formations.

These coral gardens form maze-like grottos and are homes to snappers,

Above: Blue ring angel — so named because of its blue ring behind the eyes. (Note the curve extension tusk on the gill fin.)

groupers, blow fish, box fish and coral trouts. Sharing the environment are squirrel fish, clown fish with their anemone playmates and a host of different coloured damsels, wrasse, file fish, trumpet fish and parrot fish.

Visiting predator fish like barracudas, garfish, queenfish and jacks often make their presence to feed on smaller fish. This causes panic amongst the fish, their darting to safety sends vibration through the water. You may at times hear the crackling noises of snapping shrimps hiding in coral crevices. Occasionally you can spot the crown-of-thorn starfish in juvenile purple hue and the little antennas of young lobsters protruding from holes amongst coral heads.

Dominating species of corals found here are brain corals, table corals, independent mushroom corals, staghorn corals, sponges and small patches of luminous emerald green corals. Bi-valves like the zig-zag oysters are common amongst eroded coral heads and the family of murex, cones, cowries and top shells are commonly seen.

Dive Scenes

The *northern reefs* off Nakalay Beach and Haad Yea Beach conform to slightly different formation and species of corals. A broken section of a pier built from Nakalay Beach now lies beneath the seabed. The mangled steels and concrete slabs form an artificial reef where abundant fish make their homes. Species like the Moorish idol, snappers, groupers, bat fish and coral trouts are seen in pairs. At the outskirts of this artificial reef lies brain corals and rock boulders encrusted with coralline algae and patches of young growing table corals.

Night diving here will give you an opportunity to see barracudas asleep, shrimps and spiny lobsters leaving their dens to feed and parrot fish covered with a film membrane.

About 500 metres away lies another reef off Haad Yea Beach. The seabed shows an interesting vast fringing reef formation in its different levels. The reef flat is almost 30 metres from the shore and is exposed during low tide. It comprises more of table staghorns, hump corals, mushroom corals than other species. At the deeper end on the right you will find brain corals and brittle disc corals and lettuce leaf corals on the left. On the reef slope at the deeper end, boulder corals and brain corals together with patches of soft corals are found fringing the sandy seabed.

Spotted sweetlips, snappers, surgeons and spinefoot fish favour the reef crest and reef slope area. The golden toothless trevally in pairs often visit this reef, swimming at the shallow ends to feed on fish fry. Squids frequent this dive site during the months of December to March, and mating pairs of cuttlefish can also be seen during these months.

Schools of horse mackerels often make their debut here feeding on the rich plankton while their cousin, the Indian mackerels, prefer to dart in and out of coral cays feeding on fish fry.

Above: Currently isolated, unspoilt and undeveloped — Laem Singh Beach.

On the deeper end of the reef slope roams the bigger pelagic fish and a small family of hawksbill turtle is often seen feeding on the algae found on eroded coral heads. Visibility is better at the shallow ends where there is abundant coral life. Coral reefs here almost touch the shore and reaches to a depth of 18 to 20 metres.

Because of the flat reef which extends almost to the shore, longtail boats can only beach on the shore during high or slack tide. Hence, if you are taking a break between the first and second dive on this beach, the boatman reads the residing tide and signals when to move before his boat gets grounded on the reef.

KAMALA BEACH ROCK OUTCROP AND OFF LAEM SINGH BEACH

Rock outcrops from the Andaman Sea provide good dive sites. The one located 300 metres from Kamala Beach is also a favourite amongst dive shops of Patong Beach. About 2 km away towards the northern end lies secluded *Laem Singh Beach*, with coral reefs just a few metres from the shore. These reefs offer excellent shallow dives amongst rocks and coral gardens. *Laem Singh Beach* is just a short strip of sandy shore with weather-beaten rock structures at the ends. The back drop is a steep forested hill where a few coconut palmed etiolate toward the sea. This beach is serene and its clear waters and close proximity to luxurious landscapes and seascapes capture a relaxing prevailing atmosphere. Only two makeshift food restaurants operate in the day for divers or tourists brought in by longtail boatmen.

Characteristics

Kamala site continues from a rock outcrop where underwater scenes are little caves and irregular crevices. Patch reefs are found on the eastern side facing Kamala Beach. Dive depth: 10–18 metres outer waters; and 5–8 metres inner waters.

Dive Scenes

The Kamala rock outcrop is small, however, there are lee corners for boats to anchor. Deeper dives are conducted on the outer side facing the open sea where the rocks unfurl in a tapering manner. Amongst the rocks are natural caves where snappers, cobias, sweetlips, bat fish and grunters make their homes. Sharing the surrounding waters are isolated clumps of rocks which diminish into smaller ones towards the sandy seabed. Groupers, coral trouts, parrot fish and breams roam the bottom while mullets, tunas, surgeons and schools of jacks often circle mid-water and occasionally dive to feed on fish fry.

The inner side of this rock outcrop gently slopes to a channel patch of coral reefs which extends to the brim of cliffs and small patches of isolated beaches near the headland. The coral gardens are sporadic and are dominated by colourful parrot fish families. Avoid the channel between the mainland and the rocks as prevailing currents are strong.

Characteristics

At *Laem Singh* site, a huge mass of closely-knit boulder corals form a plateau with gorges in between to attract divers to observe the marine creatures living within. Dive depth : 8 – 15 metres.

Dive Scenes

Diving off Laem Singh Beach is usually the second dive to coincide with the surface interval break time on the beach.

Although there are coral reefs just a few metres away, the deeper end on the northern point offers the required depth to inject excitement in this sport.

Boulder corals and rocks rolled from the cliffs are very close and compact, giving rise to an underwater plateau with divisions appearing like gorges. Through the years, the developing and undercurrent erosions have sculptured maze-like tunnels in between the rock and coral formations. Moray eels, damsels, lizard fish and gobies live together with groupers and grunters amongst this amazing of seabed structure. Schools of large yellow tails, rabbit fish, fox fish and angels move with the tide. Migratory squid and cuttlefish frolic, feed and mate in these waters during the months of December to February.

Sometimes the clarity is marred by the flow of silt caused by offshore tin dredging off Nai Yang and Bangtao beaches. A gradual increase of 8 to 15 metres depth prevails at this dive site.

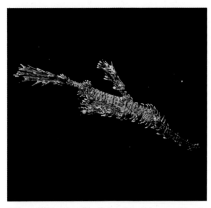

Above: This rare ghost pipe fish discovered by the brilliance of a torchlight will excite any diver.

EAST COAST OFFSHORE ISLANDS DIVE SITES

Most dive shops conduct their on-start operation of these east coast dives from the calm waters of Chalong Bay which is nearest to the dive sites. By special arrangement, dive boats can also leave from other beaches.

Above: Shark Point — one of the most popular dive sites patronized by divers.

SHARK POINT (HIN MUSANG)

Locally known as *Hin Musang*, it is the most popular dive site off the east coast. *"Hin"* in Thai means rock and this amazing outcrop which extends to the seabed displays one of the most intriguing marine ecosystems of flora and fauna. This dive site got its name because of the frequent sightings of the docile leopard shark. There is no plant life on this rock outcrop, but large numbers of sea birds roost here in the evening. This popular dive site is located 1½ hours away from Chalong Bay.

Ardent divers from dive shops and associations are wary about commercial fishing near the dive sites. They are particularly concerned about the leopard sharks which have become an attraction amongst divers. Their fear of these sharks disappearing, coral life and other fish diminishing as a result of illegal fishing have made authorities impose a ban on commercial fishing.

The site is now declared a marine sanctuary by local authorities and any form of fishing is prohibited 2,000 metres away from the rock outcrop. In future, divers will experience a wealthier underwater scenery below Shark Point.

Characteristics

Undulating rock surface manifested with coralline, hard corals and sponges. Fish feeding and glimpses of leopard

37

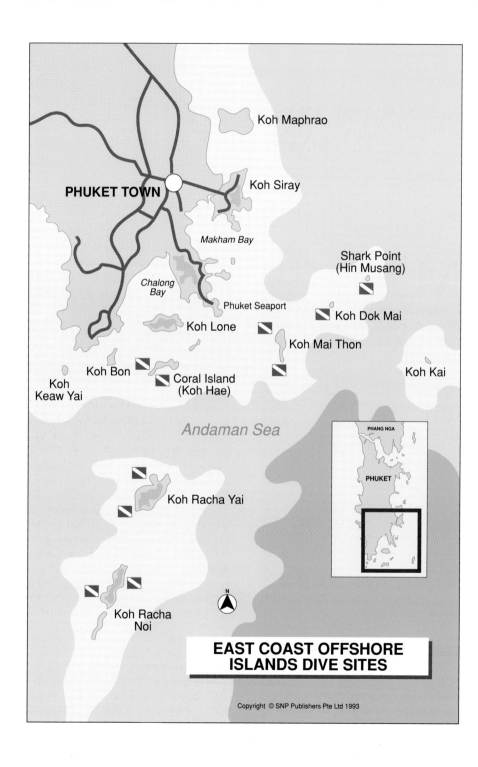

Koh Maphrao

PHUKET TOWN

Koh Siray

Makham Bay

Shark Point
(Hin Musang)

*Chalong
Bay*

Phuket Seaport

Koh Dok Mai

Koh Lone

Koh Mai Thon

Koh Bon

Coral Island
(Koh Hae)

Koh Kai

Koh
Keaw Yai

Andaman Sea

PHANG NGA

PHUKET

Koh Racha Yai

N

Koh Racha
Noi

EAST COAST OFFSHORE
ISLANDS DIVE SITES

sharks and pelagic fish are highlights.
Dive depth: 20–22 metres.

Above: Establishing a relationship with the leopard shark.

Dive Scenes

The flourishing marine ecology at *Shark Point* are well spoken of by divers. Underwater photographs of this dive site are often displayed at dive shops and these advertisements have allured many to this full-day dive program.

Your dive begins away from the crest, descending to the reef slope as you follow the dive master. When all the divers give the okay signal, the underwater tour begins. Schools of fish here are not "shy", they are used to divers because they are constantly fed by them. (Fish feeding is a good experience, just remind the operators at the beginning of the trip. Just for fun, pack yourself some cooked rice or bread in a container and put it in the B/C pocket.)

The wealth of corals and fish life here are captivating from the reef slope to the seabed. The delight will be to encounter the leopard sharks which often bask at the sandy bottom. These docile sharks, may swim away when frightened by sudden approach. Watch the dive master and he will teach you how to establish a cordial relationship. As a diver, I personally feel that establishing an acceptance relationship reveals great joy. When you have dived for many hours around these creatures you will develop your own natural way of approaching without alarming them.

But while fish feeding, you have to be wary of the bigger groupers and jacks which may take a mouthful of the bait and swim away. At this site, juvenile moray eels are an inquisitive bunch and they are brave to swim up to feed and coil around your hand. (Of course you will feel more comfortable wearing a pair of gloves.) The rich flora and fauna at this site are impressively diverse. Sponges like the Neptune-cups grow handsomely with various adjoining branches. Look out for red dotted coral trouts which just love to rest on these cups to gaze warily at you when you approach. Wrasses and damsels are the friendliest and may swim up to take a look at your mask. Snappers and pig-face breams keep a wary distance from divers. Families of angels, bat fish, surgeons and butterflies give rise to a spectrum of colours. The Moorish idol, a close relative of the surgeons, with their yellow and black strips and long white dorsals parade close to divers.

Peering into the multiple holes and small passages of brain corals, you will see shoals of cardinal fish, bigeye, vampire fish and abundant translucent fish by the schools. Venomous fish like the lion fish and stone fish are always around, but fortunately not abundant. Spot an anemone and you will come in contact with pairs of clown fish. Short antler table corals will harbour a family of black and white damsels which are fond of playing amongst the coral branches.

Above: Free living mushroom coral.

Complimenting these wonders at Shark Point are collections of gorgonian sea fans, feather stars, Christmas tree worms, sea whips, razor oysters and wing oysters which together exhibit the fascinations of shifting hues and designs. Your second dive for the day may be here or off Koh Dok Mai as it is along the route back to Chalong Bay. The program is planned by the dive master after monitoring the weather and current conditions.

KOH DOK MAI

From afar this island is shaped like a huge oblong boulder covered with vegetation. As you approach it, the sheer cliff extending to the deep sends a mixed feeling of adventure and suspense. The pale colours of this limestone karst cliff creates an impact on divers as they gaze at the height in awe before descending to discover what lies below.

Above: Koh Dok Mai's sheer cliffs extend to the seabed.

Characteristics

Deep wall and cave dive. Dive depth: 22–25 metres. Walls are rich in soft corals, sponges and abundant zig-zag oysters and other bivalves.

Dive Scenes

There are caves to explore and adjacent underwater field of sea anemone families amongst some rock gatherings. The dive master will initiate the descend via the anchor rope method and upon reaching the bottom, all divers swim towards the wall initially.

On this wall dive, carry a reliable strong torch light if you are entering the caves. Be wary of silt clouding and exercise cautious motion with your fins. Follow the lead diver and adhere to all pre-dive instructions.

Some of the caves are avenues, others run to a dead end. A few may have lights shining through, others have air vents. Unexpected encounters with big fish is common. John snappers, big Jewfish, stingrays and morays are some of the inhabitants of these caves.

Below: The amazing brilliance of yellow and black colours of a feather star.

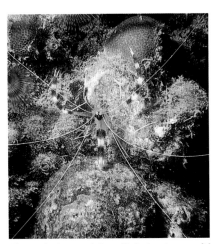

Above: A cleaner shrimp displaying its graceful antennas.

The walls of this underwater cliff is encrusted with marine flora, from soft corals, sea fans, colonies of bivalves, sponges and rich coloured encrusting coralline. Fish life is not so visible compared to *Shark Point,* but there are more caves to explore. Small groupers, yellow tail snappers, breams and wrasses are found amongst this steep wall and shoals of visiting pelagic fish roam the open waters.

An extraordinary group of sea anemone are found on some rocks at the eastern corner with large numbers of clown fish. Some have called it "anemone reef."

KOH MAI THON

This small island located one hour away from Chalong Bay was uninhabited until 1991 when a resort was built on its longest white sandy beach. Its forested hinterland of hilly terrain is home to many species of birds and insects. Their dawn and dusk cries echo through the island and this is one of the main characteristics which visitors always remember.

Dive shops do not particularly introduce the sites surrounding the island because of its lack of colours amongst what is left of its coral reef which in the past have fallen victim to illegal fishing especially dynamiting. The lack of marine life and strong currents are some of the negative factors. However, some will opt to go there, just to be acquainted with the views.

Characteristics
Sporadic reefs and evidence of reef destruction by dynamiting. Strong currents. Dive depth : 18–22 metres.

Dive Scenes
Reefs are found off the west and northern coast of the island. On the west, just off the edge of the resort are groups of brain corals and knob corals growing close to each other, forming a maze-like appearance. More fish life is seen here only in the late afternoon or during the turn of tide. Sea urchins are

Above: Twinkling reflections on the arms of a red feather star.

found in great numbers and more by colonies on sandy patches. Most of the fish found are migratory.

Off the northern coast, coral reefs in sporadic gatherings are found about 50 metres from small isolated beaches. The seabed facing the resort is mainly sandy, the water clear and ideal for swimming. A raised underwater plateau is found some 100 metres off the edge of the beach on the eastern end. The plateau is undulating and appears pale. Strong currents discourage the growth of aquatic flora or corals. The attraction here is the sighting of big fish like queen fish, jacks and barracudas which take this route to other destinations.

RACHA ISLANDS

These two islands are locally called Koh Racha Yai and Koh Racha Noi. In the Thai language *"Yai"* means big and *"Noi"* means small.

Racha Yai's attractions in diving coincide with its beautiful white sandy beaches and its surrounding palm thatched authentic cottages. When the sun is high, its dazzling white sand, tranquil clear emerald waters and back drop of evergreens project a *Robinson Crusoe* style paradise.

Racha Noi is uninhabited and the island comprises only small sandy strips and rocky cliff surroundings. It is however, a nice deserted island offering lee anchorage for diving.

Characteristics
Fringing reefs and rocky seabed. Strong currents. Dive depth : 15–28 metres. Sighting of game fish in the late afternoon, sometimes the sailfish too.

Dive Scenes
Collectively, the waters of Racha Islands are clear and deep with prevailing strong currents. It is also the playground of game fish like the magnificent sailfish, dorados, barracudas, jacks and queenfish.

Rock boulders encrusted with corals are a continuation of the cliffs. Crevices and passages in between these rocks and corals provide natural habitats for marine life. Schools of garfish roam near the surface while rabbit fish and small yellow tail snappers are abundant and feed on plankton. Blue and yellow spine unicorn fish in small shoals keep their distance, while the parrot fish, oblivious to your presence feeds greedily on algae growth amongst dead corals.

Small coves surrounding the island provide excellent shallow and interesting exploration amongst its coral formations. It is these shallow waters where you find large numbers of exotic marine and crustaceans inhabiting the coral garden. Occasionally silver breams will dart close to your mask by the shoal before vanishing into little avenues in the rocks. Squids and cuttlefish prefer the shallow waters and you see them more during the months of December to February.

These shallow reefs drop steeply to the reef crest and slopes where brain and boulder corals are found and continue sloping into the deep depth of sandy seabed. Coral reefs surrounding Racha Islands are found in narrow strips, unless they are at sheltered coves.

Live aboard diving from a *floating pantoon* is great for its stability besides other advantages. At the time of writing this book, the operators have temporarily suspended this program. Check out this dive program when you are at Chalong Bay, it may have revived again.

Above: Koh Racha Yai — an unspoilt haven for resting after a dive program.

CORAL ISLAND (KOH HAE)

This island has a fairly good reef and is nearest to the east coast of Phuket. The name *Coral Island* was given when visits to the island increased among tourists.

There are now holiday resorts, cottage-style guest houses and beach side restaurants. Hundreds of tourists visit the island during the high season and this has affected the surrounding marine life. It is still a snorkellers' paradise because the corals are close to shore. The marine life is more abundant facing the smaller beach front.

Characteristics
A garden of hard corals and rocky seabed. Dive depth : 10 – 18 metres. Aquarium fish of the smaller variety are found here.

Dive Scenes
On the deeper end of the coral reefs facing the beaches are gardens of brain, boulder and table corals growing sporadically. The increased number of visitors have not drastically defaced marine life here. Commonly sighted here are groupers, rabbit fish, spotted puffers, surgeons, butterfly, wrasses, squirrel, pipe fish, sweetlips, parrot fish and file fish. On the sandy patches, look out for the lizard fish which camouflage well, the goat fish feeling for food with its two feelers below the mouth and last but not least, spot the sand goby fish which burrows and take sand by the mouthful and throws them out.

For a change of scenes, the extreme corners of this island present jagged weather beaten rock outcrops which extends their characteristics to the seabed.

These sites are generally not sheltered and the dive boat will have to moor either farther away from these rocks or at a lee side. The sites introduce formations of eroded boulders and rocks as they are

43

constantly facing strong waves and currents. But, here is where schools of small mackerels swim to feed on plankton and their presence attract predator fish too. The rugged seabed are homes to snappers, groupers and coral trouts. Be careful of underwater currents caused by waves lashing when you are diving close to these underwater rocks.

◄ *Clown fish within the safe arms of anemone.*

PEE PEE ISLANDS (KRABI)

Pee Pee Islands are the pride of Krabi Province and besides gaining status as one of the most popular beach resorts, it is also a dive base with its own class. The islands are approximately 40 km from Krabi and its attractions of clear waters and coral reefs enjoy a healthy and well balanced natural environment for diving. Differing landscapes from hills to beaches and bays, have influenced the developments on these two islands.

Above: Songserm King Cruiser is one of the most luxurious catamaran-hull passenger cruisers offering daily trips to Pee Pee Island.

PEE PEE DON, the bigger of the two islands is blessed with a sporadic spread of fine scenic beaches around the island. Adding to this attraction are coves and bays which offer shelter for mooring. With these natural advantages, the island developed from a quiet fishing village to an island resort with modern facilities to accommodate visitors.

PEE PEE LEY, smaller and although not commercially developed because of its lack of beaches, flat land and mooring facilities, it has its own natural attractions. There are caves to explore, steep cliffs to climb and because there are no resorts, the surrounding reefs are untouched by man hence providing better dive sites.

Capitalizing on these combined attractions, tour operators have successfully promoted daily visits to the islands as one of the most popular tour packages from *Phuket* and *Krabi*. There are no other island tours during the high season with a crowd as large as 2,000 local and foreign visitors a day. During the peak season, a day's advance booking is required to assure you of a seat on the boat.

Above: Tonsai Bay of Pee Pee Island is also a rendezvous for visiting yachts.

The calm waters of the bay provide safe mooring and boats on day trips also berth here. The sea front is busy from noon to 3.00 p.m. at the pier. But as soon as the tour boats leave for Krabi and Phuket, serenity sets in through the evening till noon the following day, when scores of visitors flock to the beach.

Above: Boatman barbecues a duck during surface interval time.

To keep up with the demand for sea transfers to Pee Pee Islands, **Songserm Travel Center** introduces to its latest fleet, the ***King Cruiser***, which is a 3,000 ton catamaran-hull passenger cruiser with a capacity of 888 seats. Ensuring safety and stability at all times even if the open sea journey may sometimes turn choppy, passengers can enjoy on-board facilities like video and television, games room, a snack bar and optional air-conditioned cabins.

Pee Pee Don's diving infrastructure has gained its berth as an excellent dive base and as a diving resort. There are well equipped dive shops, a diversity of accommodation to suit your budget, choice of restaurants, mobile phones and adequate boats to facilitate diving.

You may either choose to stay and dive from the island, or join a dive program from *Krabi* or *Phuket*. From Phuket, stay-aboard diving is also a program promoted by dive shops.

Most dive shops are found on *Ton Sai Beach* which is sheltered within the bay.

Locating dive shops and game fishing operators are easy. Just walk along the little village path lined with rows of shops and you will not miss them. It is a trend that almost all dive shops operate fishing tours and it is common to see dive equipment exhibited alongside fishing gears in front of the shops.

As there are no vehicles, except a motorcycle or two for the policeman on duty, bicycles and push carts are widely used. If you are going on a dive trip from the island, your dive equipment will be loaded on push carts and the dive crew will push them to the awaiting boats by the beach.

Above: Push cart serves as means of transport for dive equipment.

Above: Longtail dive boat takes rest at Maya Bay.

When you intend to go on a dive package from Phuket, check out the details and ask the operators whether it is a total live aboard diving or is there an option to stay a night or two on the island. Arrangements are flexible. Personally, I would recommend a night or two stay on the island to experience the stunning natural beauty from dawn to dusk.

Accommodation is spread out evenly between *Ton Sai Beach* and *Loh Dahlum Beach*. You can have a choice of thatched roof bungalows with fan amongst the cool canopy of coconut palms or the luxury of air-condition rooms with modern amenities. Besides enjoying the scrumptious seafood cuisines and pleasures of diving, you can embark on hill climb to capture the panoramic view of both the bays and crescent beaches from the view point. It is easy to locate the trail by asking the friendly local people.

Krabi

The diving industry in *Krabi* is at its infant stage so there are only a few dive shops at present. Tour packages to *Pee Pee Islands* are popular and the crowd can be seen in the morning by Chao Fa Pier.

In *Krabi* town and on *Ao Nang Beach,* dive shops share the same dive sites off neighbouring islands. It takes less than an hour journey by boat from town and about half an hour from Ao Nang Beach.

Krabi Province is 2½ hours drive from Phuket and its major town activities are centred by the river banks and estuary. Fishing provides one of the major revenues for Krabi besides tourism. This quaint town has a range of business facilities from banking, tele-communications to accommodation. If you choose to stay in town to take in the sights of Krabi by the sea, stay by the riverside at **Wiang Thong Hotel** on *Uttarakit Road* for convenient access to Chao Fa Pier.

KRABI BEACHES

About five years ago, the popular beach of Krabi was *Ao Nang Beach,* located some 16 km from town. There was only a resort on the northern end which had comfortable fan and air-conditioned rooms. Adjacent on the south, were some simple thatched-roof huts by the sea. This ½ km stretch of small beach road is now filled with a dozen more colonies of budget cottages.

Nam Mao Beach is the furthest to the south, has great limestone karst scenes and an interesting steep hill climb, with an equally stunning steep descent to a hidden tidal lagoon. The locals linked this lagoon to a *legendary princess.*

▲ *A little authentic resort exists on Podak Island — excellent snorkelling amongst the coral reefs which are only a few strokes away.*

Separated by a rocky headland on the southern end of Ao Nang Beach are isolated *Riley Beach, Ao Phranang Beach* and *Nam Mao Beach.* These three beaches are cut off from Ao Nang Beach and access is only by boat. Five years ago, visitors were ferried there by longtail boats for its seclusion. Now, there are more than 100 thatched roof huts for rent and the once isolated beaches are now villages by the sea today.

Some have interpreted this lagoon surrounded by steep limestone cliffs as the legendary princess pool on a high level amongst the hills in drawings. This is a misconception for it is merely a hidden tidal lagoon, its presence created over ion years by natural erosions of land mass movements amongst limestone hills. There are many of these lagoons found amongst the 83 surrounding islands of Krabi and also in Phangnga Province.

A visit to the 75 million year-old *shell cemetery* is worth the while for there are only three such known sites in the world. The other two are located in Japan and Chicago (USA). The natural attractions of Krabi's landscapes offer a pleasant change after you have explored its dive sites.

DIVE PACKAGES FROM KRABI

Prices in dive package may vary according to the program, the duration, the type of dive boats and its facilities, but as a guideline:—

One Day Dive Program
(Pee Pee/Krabi) ....1,000–1,200 baht
(2 dives inclusive of tanks & weight belt only)
Operators ....All dive shops

KRABI'S DIVING FRATERNITY

Krabi Coral Diving
Krabi Resort, Ao Nang Beach
Krabi 81000
Tel: (075) 612161, Fax: (075) 611914

Seafan's Divers
Ao Nang Beach
Krabi 81000
Tel: (01) 7220110, (075) 612173

Tadpole Ltd
16–18 Ruen-Rudi Road
Krabi 81000
Tel: (075) 612393

Phi Phi Family Dive Centre
P.O. Box 18 Amphoe Muang
Krabi 81000
Tel/Fax: (075) 7220231

Mosquito Divers
Tonsai Bay
Pee Pee Don
Krabi 81000

Manta Diving
Tonsai Bay
Pee Pee Don
Krabi 81000

P.P. Scuba Dive Centre
Pee Pee Island
Krabi 81000
Tel: 01-7230627

Sea Frog (Thai) Diving (1987)
Pee Pee Islands
Krabi 81000

DIVE SITES OF PEE PEE ISLANDS

The recommended four dive sites around Pee Pee Islands are fairly sheltered, as they are located within coves and bays or on the lee side of rocky outcrops. *Maya Bay* and *Loh Samah Bay* dive sites are off *Pee Pee Ley, Bidah Islands* a further distance away and *Hin Pae* is the only site on *Pee Pee Don* at the eastern entrance of *Ton Sai Bay.*

Low winds blowing between the islands often cause choppy waters along on the journey to the dive sites. The dive sites are not far from each other. Marking Pee Pee Don as the starting point, the furthest dive site which is off *Bidah Islands*, takes about 35 minutes to reach under favourable weather conditions.

MAYA BAY

This bay surrounded by steep limestone cliffs is also a favourite snorkelling spot for hundreds of day trippers to Pee Pee Islands. They are brought here by tour operators usually between the hours of 2.00 p.m. to 3.00 p.m. for 30 minutes of snorkelling. Although their numbers may at times be great, this does not

bother divers at all, because the best of underwater scenes are found at deeper ends.

Above: A family of yellow fin fusilier curious over the presence of divers.

Characteristics

Patch reefs, wall and cave dive. Sailfish sighting may be possible in the late afternoon. Dive depth: 15–20 metres.

Dive Scenes

Within the bay, the calm and clear waters revealing patch reefs and schools of colourful fishes swimming in mid-water and around the coral formation

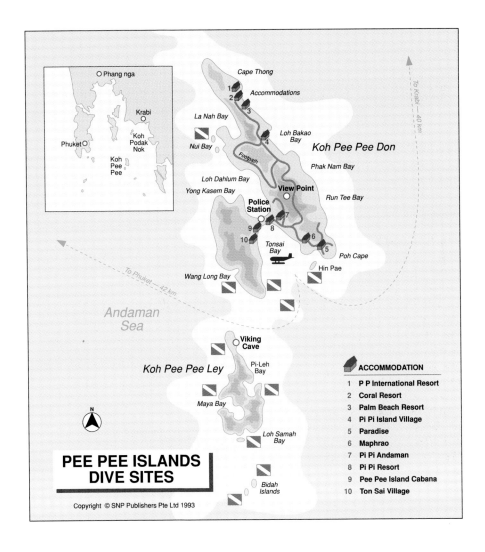

**PEE PEE ISLANDS
DIVE SITES**

ACCOMMODATION

1	P P International Resort
2	Coral Resort
3	Palm Beach Resort
4	Pi Pi Island Village
5	Paradise
6	Maphrao
7	Pi Pi Andaman
8	Pi Pi Resort
9	Pee Pee Island Cabana
10	Ton Sai Village

are snorkellers' delights. The sights and colours of marine life amongst the nooks and corners of coral formations are divers' delight.

Wall and cave dives on the northern end of the bay gives us a chance to see big pelagic fish and sea turtles. Crevices and walls at this dive site are abundant with clusters of zig-zag oysters and fan oysters. Its dense community forces some to fall on the seabed. Feather stars and wing oysters enjoy a healthy community, clinging and growing on sea whips and sea fans.

Symbiosis living between the damsels and clown fish and their anemone hosts are found amongst different coral heads. Curious groupers and coral trouts popping in and out of coral heads never fail to make themselves noticed

51

when you pass them. And if you are at the 20 metre depth range, further away from the rocks and walls, the sighting of sailfish is possible in the late afternoon when these creatures close in to feed on garfish and fish fry.

LOH SAMAH BAY

This dive site is located at the southern tip of Pee Pee Ley. The waters here is exceptionally calm because of a little islet located almost in the middle of the bay. Calm waters make gearing up easy, even on a longtail boat. Boats moor on the inner lee of the islet and divers make their way to the western end of the bay for their dive.

Characteristics

Wall and crevice dive. Abundant flora and fauna with plenty of bivalve shells attaching themselves to sea fans and corals. Dive depth: 20–22 metres.

Above: Playground rendezvous.

Dive Scenes

Descending from the western end of the bay, swim close to the wall and make your way to the open sea. On the wall is innumerable plant and animal life, with inquisitive red coral trouts, angel and butterfly fish darting around as you swim by.

About three metres before the wall ends, you will be attracted by sunlight filtering through a gorge, its steep walls plastered with prolific soft corals, seafan and coralline algae. It is large enough for the diver to swim through and the distance is about 30 metres.

BIDAH ISLANDS

This is the furthest dive site from Pee Pee Don and is located south of Pee Pee Ley. These two strange limestone sea rock outcrops which rises steeply look like a pair of army boots.

Above: Approaching Bidah Islands on a longtail boat.

Both these outcrops are close to each other, having sheer cliffs, but differing in its natural vegetation. The inner island nearer Pee Pee Ley has luxurious green vegetation, while the outer island has sporadic gray looking vegetation. This difference is distinct as you approach the site. Perhaps the natural

52

explanation surrounds the lack of top soil on the outer island which results in an unhealthy state of plant life.

Characteristics
Wall dives, sporadic coral patches on seabed. Dive depth: 18–30 metres.

Above: Flowery white and red soft corals decorate the sea walls.

Dive Scenes
The eastern side of the inner island is a good site to begin as the concentration of coral life is greater. At the deeper end, corals appear dull but are more colourful within the depths from 18 to 20 metres. The walls at certain sections appear in tiers due to erosion over the years and the seabed is undulating.

Squids gather in schools close to the walls, awaiting to feed on fish fry and smaller fish dart around feeding on plankton carried down by currents. Octopuses are found here amongst the rocky seabed close to the concentration of corals. Approach them slowly because they can be great subjects to study when they camouflage. Be careful of abundant sea urchins on the seabed.

Puffer fish and porcupine fish appear to be more curious here than other dive sites and often trail divers closely. It is quite often that divers catch up with this slow swimmer, hold it by the tail and watch it puff into a spiky ball.

HIN PAE
This dive is often programmed as the last dive on the return journey to Pee Pee Don. Its depth of 10 to 15 metres makes it favourable after completing deeper dives. Another reason is that is nearer to home base on Pee Pee Don and this encompasses a good feeling amongst the dive crews after a good day's dive program.

Surrounding this site is a broad base rock outcrop tapering gradually to a seabed of reef formations. The shallow ends are favourite sites for snorkellers, while divers take on deeper depths.

Characteristics
A good example of a coral reef formation illustrating reef flat, reef crest and reef slope of a fringing reef is found here. Between the fringing reef and seabed are patch reefs of brain and antler corals forming the base of this rock outcrop. Dive depth: 10–15 metres.

Dive Scenes

Your dive begins at the deeper end and you descend in between the patch reef and the main fringing reef.

Above: A wealth of hard and soft corals of an undisturbed shallow reef.

Boulder and brain corals form the main species amongst the patch reef. Growing from eroded heads and corners of these corals are table corals and at times small clusters of blue tip antler corals. Sea anemone growing on coral heads and bases between boulders play hosts to inquisitive damsels and clown fish. There are flowery soft corals in hues of purple and orange closer to the reef slope. Ascend to the reef crest of hard corals and check out the numerous holes and interconnecting passage ways which are homes and avenue routes to small aquarium fish and crustaceans. Cleaner wrasse, damsels, angels, butterflies, boxing shrimps, cleaner shrimps and small lobsters inhabit this section of the reef. This variable undulating seascapes offer an opportunity to study the different formations of a fringing reef.

This dive site is excellent for night dive because the current is not strong and offers a good chance to see nocturnal marine creatures leaving their lairs to feed and play.

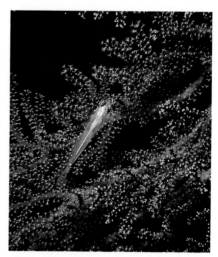

Above: Asleep safely in the arms of sea fan.

DIVE SITES OF KRABI

A concentration of small islands with artistic limestone features and rock outcrops are located one hour by longtail boat from Krabi Town and about 30 minutes from Ao Nang Beach. Fringing reefs and reef patches surrounding these land masses offer excellent diving and snorkelling.

Above: Longtail boat takes rest on gin clear waters off Chicken Island.

The coastal waters off *Podak Island* and *Chicken Island* are blessed with a spread of reef flats just a few strokes from the beach. Coral formations are found at a 3 to 6 metres depth and are excellent sites for snorkelling.

The dazzling white sand of *Podak Island's* curve beach can be seen from *Ao Nang Beach* and it stands out more on a bright sunny day. Only a few huts are erected here and a thatched roof restaurant serves the needs of the guests.

Chicken Island is named because of its irregular high rocky hills which form an image of a chicken. Only small patches of beaches dot the coast. A sand bank on its north eastern tip connects to an islet called *Koh Tub*, its clear sapphire blue waters on either side of the bank stands brilliantly surrounding the white sand. Although deep dive sites are not found near these two islands, they offer excellent landscapes, the restaurant on Podak Island is the rest venue for divers before their second dive.

KOH MAE URAI

Although called an island, *Koh Mae Urai* is a mass of weather-beaten rock outcrops rising from the sea. Its lime

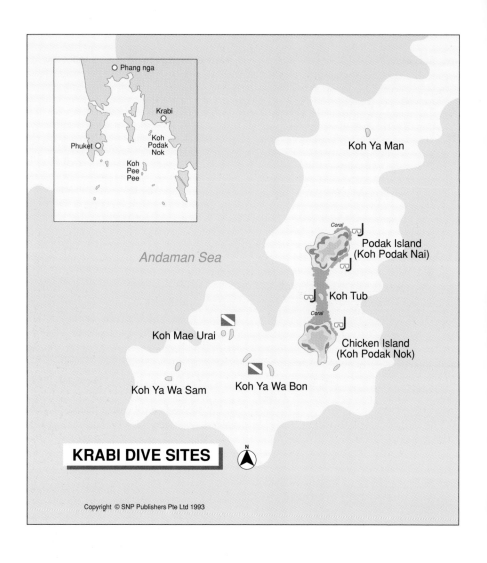

stone base, through the years of winds and rainfalls have exposed a composition of rustic colours on the cliffs, depicting a beautiful colossal mural. There are numerous small outcrops which provide excellent mooring for longtail boats.

Characteristics

Irregular eroded rock diving with small archways and labyrinth to explore, however, fish life is not abundant and coral life, scanty. Dive depth: 15–18 metres.

Dive Scenes:
Even if there is a strong wind blowing on the outside, these sheltered areas are calm which makes gearing up easy. The visibility in this site largely depend on tidal factors. However, visibility is best at peak tide when the current is slack.

Above: A well suited name to this island on account of its landscape — Chicken Island.

Fish life here is not abundant, but you will be accompanied by the common parrots and wrasses around. Sporadic spread of patch boulder corals and pore corals support the growth of sea anemone and a host of clown and damsel fish. Schools of young barracudas are common as they circle mid-water for their prey. Roaming on the seabed of coral chips and sand are goat fish and breams, occasionally swimming close to take a look at you out of a host of antler corals.

Because of a rich flow of plankton in the waters, the base of the outcrops are studded with zig-zag oysters. Another unique feature of this underwater limestone architecture is its layered formation caused by currents and waves.

Hence, the top masses are supported by smaller base with eroded structures like a mushroom.

KOH YA WA BON

Dive sites off this uninhabited rock outcrop formations give illusions of imaginary figures. Its sheer cliffs and jagged rock characteristics extends to the seabed and its multiple adjoining

Above: Sea cucumbers amidst fire corals.

57

smaller rock surfaces out of the water to act as wind breakers. Hence, there are a few choices to moor the boat.

Characteristics

Fish life is more abundant here and the spotting of reef sharks is common. There are limestone archways and grottos. Dive depth: 8–15 metres.

Dive Scenes

When you descend, you will encounter schools of yellow tail fish and green damsels. On the seabed, bottom fish dwellers are not abundant, however, do not be surprised if black tip reef sharks tail you from a distance. Most of them are fat and well fed, but display a curious and territorial instinct.

You could swim around this massive rock structure and there are at least 3 good passage ways to swim through. These swim throughs are the added adventure in diving, for your chances of encountering predator fish are good as these swim throughs are its' usual swimming pattern. Exercise caution in swimming around these area, as there are sharp barnacles on the rocks.

▲ *Horse eye jacks in frenzy feeding on plankton.*

SIMILAN ISLANDS

Divers charmed by the fantasies of the Similan Islands acclaimed that the myriad dive locations reflect some of the world's best. Veteran divers of the *Andaman Sea*, describe the aquatic flora and fauna as the richest and most diverse collections within the inner space of the sea.

Above: An "aquatic inflorescence" of sea fans and soft corals.

Its astounding underwater architecture include caves, mazes of swim-through gorges, underwater boulder pile-ups leading to adventurous drop-offs, sloping reefs and vast coral gardens. Migratory pelagic fish like the graceful manta rays, giant jacks, barracudas and the gentle whale sharks so often reveal their presence to avid divers, as they parade through the silent deep. And equally fascinating on the islands are rocky terrains where some tower to great heights, in artistic forms jutting out to the edge of the sea. The backdrop of isolated dense tropical greens throw a blanket of contrast to the landscapes and together they introduce the immense attractions of the Similan Islands seascapes and landscapes.

SIMILAN DIVE SITES
Almost all boats leave in the evening for the Similans and sometimes in an unscheduled convoy. Across the Andaman Sea on a dark, starry or full moon night, the boat captains keep in touch by radio and yarn through the journey. Keeping abreast of each boat's position is a safe way and greatly encouraged.

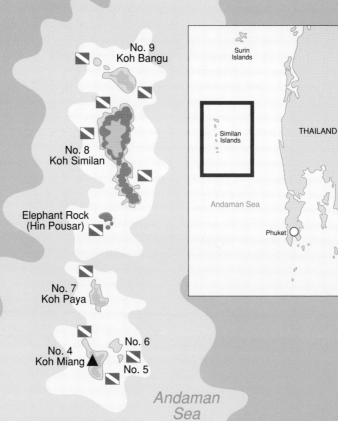

No. 9
Koh Bangu

No. 8
Koh Similan

Elephant Rock
(Hin Pousar)

No. 7
Koh Paya

No. 4
Koh Miang

No. 6

No. 5

*Andaman
Sea*

Similan National Marine Park
Office & Camping Site

No. 3
Koh Payang

No. 2
Koh Payang

No. 1
Koh Huyong

Surin
Islands

THAILAND

Similan
Islands

Andaman Sea

Phuket

SIMILAN ISLANDS DIVE SITES

There is no fixed program or pattern on how the dives will be conducted around the archipelago. The dive personnel in charge would have planned the pattern according to his preference which he feels is best for the divers. In the open sea, prevailing weather may change dive plans from one site to another, preferably in favour of a lee mooring.

However, one of the most common dive patterns adopted by most operators is to start diving from the north at Island No. #8 and #9 and work down south to Island No. #1 which is nearest to Phuket.

By the time the boat moors in the calm bay of Island No. #8, it will still be dark morning, with 2 to 3 hours before dawn breaks.

ISLAND NO. #8 (KOH SIMILAN) AND NO. #9 (KOH BANGU)

A great start of this dive expedition begins on the calm bay of *Island No. #8*. In fact, just when you are brushing your teeth and gazing into the gin clear waters, you will see a gathering of breams, surgeons and damsel fish darting near the surface in search of food. Combined with views of patch corals, these natural phenomenon will trigger your urge to make your first dive.

And as you gaze on yonder to the pristine white sandy beach, you will be equally spellbound by artistic rocks and boulders towering to great heights from the headland.

At Island No. #8, the single huge triangular boulder is awe-inspiring and is the **symbolic landmark of the Similans** in many postcards and dive brochures. Getting to the beach is a part of the expedition program and you may hike up this rock to enjoy a sweeping view of the beach.

Above: Branching staghorn corals a common shallow reef builder.

On **Island No. #8 (Koh Similan)**, the best dive site is at the *Fantasy Reef* located off the mid western side of this island. This reef has a bounteous collection of marine flora and fauna and the depth averages around 25 metres.

In shades of pink, red, orange and purple, the soft floral corals sway and droop on the walls of coral heads and rocks. Stacks of zig-zag oysters overcrowding the walls have their shells encrusted with coats of orange hue living corals. The distinct shapes of table corals join the garden structure, with clusters of staghorn aloof at variable corners. Pore coral heads play hosts to bivalves and brightly Christmas tree worms that pop into the safety of

Above: Taking leave from diving, divers scale up to the famous rock of Island No. #8 for a majestic view of the bay.

Stray away from the reef and you will encounter the more pelagic fish like jacks, barracudas, tunas, rainbow runners and queenfish. Occasional schools of tunas swimming by, block off the light and cast a great shadow over the reef, causing temporary confusion amongst the marine life.

Island No. #9 (Koh Bangu)

The dive site on the north western tip of this island between some rock outcrops offer a comfortable depth of between 10 to 15 metres of adventure diving. Divers refer to this site as *"Christmas Point"*.

There are challenging swim-throughs amongst the rock formations which add to the main attraction of this site. The sightings of pelagic fish like the barracudas, jacks, trevally and queenfish are likely as they turn predators on smaller fish amongst the rock formations and crevices. These predator fish are more active when there is current, as this natural phenomenon stimulates their appetite to feed. The unfurling and stacking rock formation tapers away to a plain coral reef with mounts of patch corals and a healthy growth of hanging purplish soft corals.

This dive site edges the open sea and increases your chance of encountering the majestic silent and graceful manta rays, constantly flapping its wings as it cruises agape feeding on plankton rich waters. The enormous whale sharks can occasionally be seen swimming close to underwater drop-offs.

After your second dive, the boat returns to Island No. #8 for mooring. This would probably be the site for the rest of the day and going ashore is part

the pores when startled. Coralline and sponges spread over the surface of almost all rocks. The spread of orangy red gorgonian sea fans reach to an enormous size of almost two arms length and black corals grow in healthy clusters.

Groupers, trouts and snappers play hide and seek amongst the maze of coral formations while damsels frolic amongst protuberance of table corals. Angels and bat fish parade in and out of crevices and the swift swimming trigger fish scout around divers curiously. The dominance of trigger fish decreases the population of sea urchins, as it is their favourite food. Thus, a minimum of these prickly urchins are found at this dive site.

of the program. You can attempt to scale the heights of the symbolic rock on this island and it will not be difficult as there are tracks, wooden rails and ropes to assist the climb.

Night diving is usually done at the northern headland of this bay. It is advisable to stay within the bay limits to avoid the strong current. Shallow waters amongst rock crevices and coral beds in the night introduces a great variety of sleeping fish like parrots and damsels. Other rewarding sights will be nocturnal animals like lobsters and shells.

Above: The rock that gave the site its name — Elephant Rock. Novice and veterans vote the sea garden to be one of the very best of Similans.

ELEPHANT HEAD ROCK OUTCROP (HIN POUSAR)

If you wonder where this rock outcrop got its name, look closely when you go there. The seabed beneath and surrounding this rock have been rated as one of the best in the regions.

The surface of this rock tapers gradually and steeply at different sides to the seabed in a show of unusual rock formations. There are crevices, caves, swim throughs, big holes and terracing features amongst these underwater natural architecture where abundant marine life make their homes.

Complementing the site is a spread of colourful hard and soft corals, some hanging like chandeliers of the deep. Others take the shapes of tables, staghorns, elkhorns, cups and brains. Amongst the canopy of these corals are exotic aquarium fish collections flashing luminous bright blues, yellows and red colours. Shrimps, prawns, little crabs and tiny lobsters share this natural habitat with the fish.

Concentrating on a small area at a time will give you the opportunity to notice the great variety of living creatures of the deep. Hasty fin strokes will deprive you of this chance.

If you are armed with a video or camera, the numerous big holes make very attractive *"photo frames"* when you peer through and someone else takes the picture. Side winding through caves and gorges is simply great and you will be thrilled with all the fish encounters along the way.

When you encounter the emperor and blue ringed angel fish, they often dart around you to ward you off. Groupers merely gaze curiously, damsels peep through crevices, clown fish seek shelter in the tentacles of the anemone, while the lethargic lion fish, fans its pelvic fins oblivious to your presence. Sea turtles encircle divers at a safe distance and draw nearer when divers are in small groups of two or three.

The second dive is usually at the same site because there is so much more to see. After this, the dive boat heads towards Island No. #4 for mooring.

Above: Diver enjoying the thrills of a swim through.

ISLAND NO. #4 (KOH MIANG)

After taking in the splendour of the deep blues at Elephant Rock, the dive boat now moors in the calm waters of the eastern bay at Island No. #4 facing Island No. #5.

Divers are taken ashore to relax in the afternoon as the crew goes ashore on Island No. #4 to collect fresh water and dispose off their accumulated garbage in a centralized pit.

This is the only inhabited island in the Similans which the *National Marine Park Authorities* have allocated camp

sites and bungalows for rent. There is a quaint restaurant serving hot food and beverages here. During the peak season the restaurant is open everyday, but only over the weekend during the off peak season.

On Island No. #4, the walk to the camp site area takes about 10 minutes through a cool canopy of rain forest. The path is distinct and the trail runs across a stream where attractive creepers and ferns are found along the way. The sound of insects and birds are apparent and is certainly a natural spot to bird watch in the early morning. You may opt to stay for a night on this island after checking with your dive master.

Above: A gift of underwater colours.

Before your dive the next morning, try waking up early to catch the sunrise. Sunrise in the Similans has its distinct beauty and that is one of the bonuses of the trip.

The tranquil clear blue waters on this eastern site introduces divers to a vast serene seabed of white sand and sporadic coral patches. Gradual terracing, with undulating formation of the seabed makes this dive very pleasant with visibility of 25-30 metres.

You will be able to spot schools of fish approaching in these clear waters. Fish common in this reef are jacks, barracudas, groups of parrot fish, stray snappers and solitary black tip sharks at deeper waters.

Above: The emperor angel – "dressed" in royal colours.

After you have enjoyed the deeper waters, check out the shallow areas near the shores for moray eels to feed. These ferocious looking moray eels, belie their placid nature. You can feed them and stroke them after building a relationship. Where possible, tuck a few strands of squid tentacles in your B/C pocket during this dive. They are chewy and holds better when you are feeding the moray eels.

Your second dive can be challenging one that tests a diver's patience and skill before the rewards of a captivating reef. On the northern point at the apex of the landscape, there is a drop of 25 metres to a sandy seabed. Strong currents prevail and divers must work their way 45° North East for about 10 minutes across sandy beds before sighting an isolated large area of corals and rock formations encrusted with gorgeous sea fans, Neptune whips, cups, wing oysters, zig zag bivalves and a host of anemone fish and other exotic coloured coral fish.

Above: The clown trigger – one of the most beautiful of its species.

Night diving is conducted at Island No. #4 on the eastern site as there are less currents and no huge boulders or maze like rock structures which may sometimes confuse divers at night dive. Sleeping parrots and puffers are good subjects of photography and the sightings of spiny lobsters (dark brown species) are common as they venture out of their lairs to feed.

65

ISLAND NO. #7 (KOH PAYU)

The following morning if you wish to see more black tip sharks, take a plunge at Island No. #7. Remember that black tip sharks are territorial and its behaviour may sometimes react with cautious and swift aggressive movements. It is best to stick close to each other if you do not have the experience with sharks, or if this is going to be your first encounter in the wild. There are abundant fish to keep the sharks well fed and they are not aggressively hungry.

The rocky cliffs of this island at the northern tip tapers into the deep. The constant back wash of waves give little chance of coral growth, except barnacles and oysters. At the deeper end, marine flora begins, although not at an impressive rate. There are lots of yellow tails, the small blue and yellow snappers, big wrasses, parrots and spotted sweetlips fish which make their homes between the rocks.

Black tip sharks swim in languid grace amongst the fish without causing alarm and I have often wondered when is their feeding time. It is a rare sight to see sharks in the wild attacking and feeding on other fish. I have had only one opportunity to see three 1½ metre black tip sharks feeding on a school of fish fry which were easy victims.

The boat will return to Island No. #5 for an adventurous drift diving before mooring for the night in the sheltered bay of Island No. #4.

ISLAND NO. #1 (KOH HUYONG)

Dives at this island are usually the last two before the boat heads for Phuket as the variable shallow depths are most comfortable. It is also the closest island to Phuket.

The seabed configurations comprises coral gardens teeming with a great variety of marine life at a depth of 10 to 15 metres. These shallow waters, permitting the sun rays to penetrate, creates a healthy prolific ecosystem of the most colourful nature. The colour of hard and soft corals and sea fans display seven guiding colours. There are apple green algae with round leaves drooping over the ledge of rocks over encrusting crimson coralline algae.

The bigger pelagic fish are not abundant here, but the dive site attractions are dominated by reef fish commonly seen in aquariums. The anemone clown fish and its cousin, the tomato clown grazes and mingles around the stinging tentacles of their host anemone. The luminous blue stripe gobies hover around the brain corals, while active reticulated striped damsels dash amongst antler corals. Angel and bat fish parade in schools while the trigger clown fish prefer to be in pairs or single. Cleaning wrasse catches the eye of divers, as they are often seen swimming in and out of the bigger fishes' gaping mouth and picking on morsels of food. Its emerald coloured cousin, the swallow tail lunar wrasse do not shy away when you attempt to feed the fish. They will be one of the first to take the bait from your hand.

Fish feeding may not be a prime program on the expedition and if your dive buddies share the same interest, you are bound to get a lot of fun out of it. Boiled rice which disperse in flakes to attract fish are easily available from the boat. Bread is another substitute, however, they disintegrate fast in the water.

If you plan to feed fish, I would suggest you use squid or cuttlefish, because their chewy texture makes it harder for the feeders to chew off. This prolongs your feeding time and attracts a greater variety of fish.

The boat sets for base in Phuket around noon. The return journey usually sets in a melancholic note when all divers gather and exchange notes, addresses for a possible rendezvous in Phuket on their next dive holiday to the *Similans*.

Above: A timid dog-face puffer.

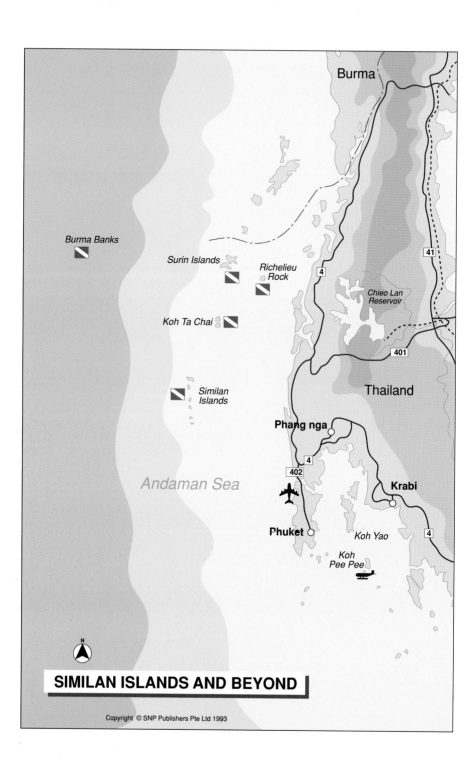

Burma

Burma Banks

Surin Islands

Richelieu
Rock

41

4

Chieo Lan
Reservoir

Koh Ta Chai

401

Similan
Islands

Thailand

Phang nga

4

Andaman Sea

402

Krabi

Phuket

Koh Yao

4

Koh
Pee Pee

N

SIMILAN ISLANDS AND BEYOND

BEYOND THE SIMILANS
TO THE BURMA BANKS

This chapter introduces a new horizon to adventure scuba diving in the *Andaman Sea* from Phuket. Although the *Similan Islands* is renowned as one of the world's best diving destinations, the diving fraternity in Phuket have ventured beyond to chart new dive locations and sites as additional programs.

Dive sites in the *Burma Banks* and off *Surin Islands* is the talk of the town and an adventurous 7–9 day dive expedition is the latest live aboard dive tour package. The dive sites include the *Similan Islands, Burma Banks, Richelieu Rocks* off *Surin Islands* and *Koh Ta Chai*. Highlights of this expedition include diving with sharks, sightings of whale

▲ *Divers admiring the gentle giant (whale shark) of Richelieu Rock. (Photo Courtesy by Mark Strickland)*

sharks, manta and a probable chance of witnessing shark feeding if all influencing factors are in favour. (Not all dive operators share the idea of shark feeding).

However the program may vary according to weather conditions as the open sea is sometimes rough in the tropics.

Dive operators are still cautious in introducing dives beyond the Similans to the Burma Banks, because of the long journey which currently most dive boats require refuelling. Tropical storms in the open sea are unpredictable and dive boats of at least 20 metres can face the rough sea. The **M.V. Fantasea** of **Fantasea Divers** was amongst the pioneers which have done reconnaissance dives, charted the sites for dive expedition to the *Burma Banks*.

Besides the *M.V Fantasea*, two sailing boats, the *Crescent* and *Seraph* from **S.E.A. Yacht Charter** and *Sai Mai II* of **Siam Diving Center** are also conducting dive packages to *Burma Banks* currently.

Fantasea Divers of Phuket pioneered one of the first dive trips to the Burma Banks as early as 1990. But the routes and dive packages were only commercially viable in 1991 when divers' comfort and safety were taken into consideration.

THE EXPEDITION PROGRAM GUIDELINE

Most dive operators would prefer all divers to hand in their dive bags and personal effects in the afternoon for their crew to transfer them to the dive boat. Departure is in the evening around 7.00 to 8.00 p.m for the first leg of the journey to the *Similan Islands*, arriving there early next morning.

Two dives will be conducted at selected sites as an introduction to the marine wonders of the Andaman Sea. A possible night dive is conducted and if weather permits the 10 hours to the *Burma Banks* begins.

Above: The steel hull M.V. Fantasea dive boat.

The boat will stay in the open sea of these banks for one or two days, depending on the weather. Two or three day dives will be conducted per day, but night dive is not permitted as these waters are homes to the silver tip sharks.

The dive operator who conducts shark feeding, studies the weather and flow of current and also the behaviour of the silver tip sharks before commencing the shark feeding underwater.

After experiencing adventure diving at *Burma Banks*, the boat leaves for *Surin Islands*, about 6 hours away. Some boats may arrive there in the morning, others in the afternoon and this largely depends on what time they take off from the banks.

Surin Islands offer basically a resting place at its calm bays, as the favourite diving sites are located off *Richelieu Rocks* which is about 1½ hours away. Most whale sharks and manta rays are spotted here. If there are enough of them around, the program to stay for another day to encounter these awesome marine creatures may follow.

The next destination is *Koh Ta Chai*, some 2 hours away for day diving before commencing a return journey to the *Similan Islands* for the remaining available dives for a night to two before returning to Phuket in the afternoon.

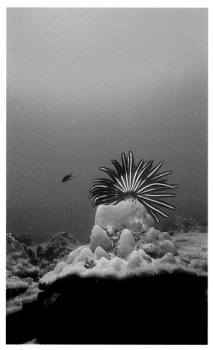

Above: A solitaire feather star on top a pore coral mount.

THE BURMA BANKS DIVE SITES

The *Burma Banks* are open water giant sea mounts which rise dramatically 70 to 300 metres from the seabed up to 16 to 18 metres from the surface. These banks measure from as small as the size of 2 football fields to approximately 3 sq km plateau like structures with gradual and sheer drop offs. Although they are considered raw open reefs to divers, there is evidence of fish dynamiting and some areas are more obvious than others.

Inspite of this act by man, the plankton rich waters with sporadic spread of coral mounts support a wealth of marine life, especially the pelagic fish.

Visibility exceeding 30 metres is one of the rewarding factors in these vast banks. The other enlightening scenes would be the healthy growth of juvenile corals, especially the staghorn species. As this growth cycle continues, the greater number of marine life will return.

There are more than a dozen banks covering a vast area for divers to explore. Some have been charted, others are still left unexplored. Records have shown that the average depth in these open water reefs on the banks is between 15 to 20 metres and its drop-offs can reach 300 metres and more.

There are sporadic old coral mounts which supports the growth of sponges and coralline algaes. Masses of staghorn corals are seen more on the edge of the slopes amidst small mounts of pore corals. Coral debris as a result of fish dynamiting are not totally without marine life. Its piles, although loosely formed, supports the smaller crustaceans and fish like wrasses and gobies.

71

Above: White spotted puffer trailing a golden puffer in gin clear waters at the Burma Banks.

Of fish life, the banks attraction for divers is the opportunity to swim with sharks. There are silver tips and nurse, with hammerhead and tiger sharks occasionally appearing. In most instances, divers feel a greater sense of adventure sighting sharks than other pelagic fish.

The dog tooth and bonito tunas are common in these waters you may sometimes see the great yellow fin tuna along the slopes and steep drops. Rainbow runners and jack fish are amongst some of the midwater swimmers. Resident fish like the snappers, triggers and sweetlips are found where corals gather, especially under the table and boulder

Above: Practical dive platform enhances the comforts of dive operation.

72

corals, which have holes and small crevices for them to reside. The pig face bream and goat fish are resident fish of the staghorn corals. The terraced slopes with vertical and horizontal cave-in and crevices are homes to trigger fish fry and the moray eels.

But there are more than just these marine creatures, for upon each dive, something new and extraordinary is always discovered by different divers.

SURIN ISLANDS DIVE SITES

Richelieu Rocks

Depth : Between 15 to 30 metres

Coral Life : Soft corals, sea fans, sea whips, sponges and coralline algae grow profusely on the surfaces and base of rock boulders.

Fish Life : Sightings of whale sharks, manta rays, schools of barracudas, titan triggers, scorpion fish, stone fish, oriental sweetlips and groupers. Cuttlefish mating is a possible sighting from late November to February. (Abandoned fish traps and torn fishing nets are found amongst the rocky seabed)

Visibility is fair between 5 to 10 metres at variable depths due to rich plankton. This accounts for plankton feeders like whale sharks and the manta rays at these dive site.

Koh Ta Chai

Depth : Vary from 16 to 24 metres on the rocky surfaces and a depth of 30 metres off the slopes.

Coral Life : Abundant soft corals, sea fans, sea whips, small brittle table corals and pore corals.

Fish Life : Shoals of fish fry gather by the *"clouds"* at coral heads, cave-ins and crevices. Groupers, snappers and jacks darting around and feeding on these fry. Barracudas, yellow backs, fusiliers and green damsels swim at mid waters.

The visibility is about 8 to 12 metres with a constant rift of current and a thick film of plankton to keep the community of fish healthy and growing.

Above: Author attempts to feed an adult moray eel.

Above: Sometimes rubber dinghy takes over the dive operation when dive boats are moored in calm waters and dive sites are located away from the lee.

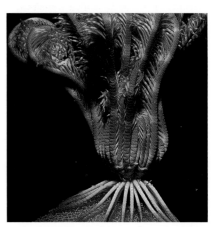

Above: The grace of a feather stars' feet and arms.

FEATURE STORY

SHARK FEEDING AT THE BURMA BANKS

It was the adventure of shark feeding that attracted me to the Burma Banks. On 16 November 1992, I boarded the *M.V. Fantasea* from Patong Bay (Phuket) with a group of cosmopolitan divers on this dive expedition. *Mark Strickland* was the cruise director and *Suzanne Forman*, the dive master. That evening as we cruised away at 9.00 pm, the subject on shark feeding was discussed and Mark said that swimming with sharks will be one of the highlights of diving at the Burma Banks but the shark feeding program will largely depend on the weather, the flow of the current and the temperament of the silver tip sharks.

However, on this trip, shark feeding was conducted and I had the opportunity to record the sequence on video and camera. Some divers may disagree with shark feeding and I respect their personal opinions. But for those who wish to experience this adventure, this story will leave you with less questions.

We arrived at the northern point of the banks on the morning of the 18 November after a 10-hour night cruise from the Similan Islands. Adventure filled our three daylight introductory dives as we were constantly escorted by

nurse and juvenile silver tip sharks, besides other pelagic fish. The vast reefs in these open waters delivered a deeper sense of inner space feelings and the drop-offs, where the awesome fish lurks, were added thrills.

Fresh Fish Baits
The next morning we did a dive at **Big Bank** (named by *Fantasea Divers* but may be called by another name by others) and preparation for shark feeding began. Mark indicated to me that he and Suzanne were going to troll for fish to feed the silver tip sharks, as they are fussy eaters and prefer fresh meat.

They were going to troll from a rubber dinghy powered by an outboard engine with hand held fishing lines. I expressed the urge to follow the team and permission was granted. I braced myself on the bow with a camera on one hand as the dinghy raced out to the open waters.

Mark had a special stainless steel trolling plate which was meant to bring the lure down deeper and when there is a strike, the contraption technically assists in hauling the fish up. Suzanne was equipped without the special gadget.

After 25 minutes of exciting trolling, Mark had 7 strikes and hauled in a small

Above: Mark and Suzanne in trolling action for dog-tooth tuna as sharks' bait.

bonito tuna, a one kilo rainbow runner and five handsome dog-tooth tunas, each weighing close to 5 kilograms; the size which Mark was aiming to bag. The catch was sufficient and the dinghy raced back to the awaiting dive boat which was rearing to go to the **Silver Tip Bank** for the shark feeding program.

After unloading the fish on the boat, Mark filleted some of the tuna for dinner and cut the rest in suitable proportions and put them into a tight lid container filled with sea water.

When we arrived at the rendezvous site, Mark briefed all divers with the aid of a dive map. The map indicated that the mooring line is secured to a boulder coral and that all divers are to swim to a nearby table coral for shelter during shark feeding, which will be conducted 6 metres away by Mark and Suzanne on this trip.

The usual gearing up conversation seemed to have mellowed before this dive. When Suzanne assisted Mark with the full arm protective sleeve, a short moment of silence followed. And like the others, I had a load of questions to ask, but withheld and found most of the answers during the dive.

I was the last diver to get into the waters and that gave me the sweeping view of pre-shark feeding scenes as I descended slowly with a video camera activated on my hand. The shark feeding pair were in position and there were juvenile silver tip sharks swimming robustly, sensing it was meal time. I remained at the base of the mooring line about 2 metres side ways from the table coral. I was in a favourable position to observe facial reactions of divers and a distant closer to the shark feeders.

When all divers were in position, Mark opened the lid, pulled out a piece of tuna and promptly placed it about a metre from his long fins. Immediately

Above: Preparing the sharks' feed.

76

the hungry snappers, triggers, breams, nurse sharks and young silver tip sharks charged for the feed. The nurse sharks being bigger had their jaws on the tuna bait first, yanking, chewing and tossing bits and pieces around which were devoured by the other fish. The pair of divers were almost clouded by fish when some of the pieces landed close to them. At times when the nurse sharks got too close, Mark had to shove them away with his hands to have a clear view of adult silver tips approaching.

The other divers watched the action intensely, expressing goggled eyed reactions as I had my video shifting from one scene to another. The frenzy feeding and the flow of the current carrying the scent of fresh fish bait had attracted the adult silver tips from the deep.

Mark and Suzanne strained their vision towards the drop-offs and through the video I saw some blur vision of white spots "dancing" and in a few seconds, I sighted 4 awesome silver tips advancing swiftly in zig zag stance. Before I could take another gulp of air, they were already swimming in circles around the pair of divers. When their swift movements stopped and as they swam around in languid grace, all the divers had their eyes glued at their swimming patterns.

All feeding stopped now and Mark had the lid tightly closed, studying the behaviour of the silver tips. This observation is important before taking out the fish bait. Sensing that the silver tips were not too excited, Mark took another piece of fish out and immediately closed the lid. He waved the fish bait to attract the silver tips, but the other fish came for the bait too.

The pair had to occasionally push the other fish away when the silver tips were moving in closer. (At this point, a careless snapper engrossed in feeding became victim to one of the silver tips) The silver tips were not greedy, but remained wary and occasionally swam close to the bait, as though sniffing it and swam off. The leader of the pack, a female measuring 2 metres called this bluff thrice and had us anticipating when it was going to take the bait.

The silver tips swam over the table coral and all divers followed their movements. Holding on to the mooring line with no cover over my head, I had a few exciting moments when they swam a little too close for comfort. But I had the thrill of looking closely at the jaw line and pale bodies of the sharks when they swam above my head.

Just when all seemed routine, a male silver tip moved in from behind Suzanne and Mark alerted her and she swung around and pushed the shark away with a shark stick. It lowered its pectoral fin, arched its diaphragm and side winded towards me, almost a metre to the video camera. I raised my shark stick and it swam over the table coral.

A few seconds after this drama, the leader of the pack decided to close in on the bait from Mark's right side. As it was about a metre away, it opened its jaws, and closed in on the bait, then took it away effortlessly as I watched Mark's hand resist once under those powerful jaws. Gracefull it swam away, reopened its mouth to crunch and I could hear the teeth crushing the fish bone. In two efforts, the entire fish bait disappeared into its stomach.

That was the action which we had been waiting for almost 30 minutes. And as though it was like an end of a "show" the other silver tips followed the leader and swam away from us to the drop-off. At this point, Mark and Suzanne swam towards us and signalled those with 500 psi on their gauges to ascend. Although we were only 30 minutes at 15 metres, the excitement caused some of the divers to use up more air.

I remained with other divers for another 15 minutes, swimming around the perimeter of the shark feeding 'arena' and at the moment without the adult silver tips around, the dive seemed so sedated.

Witnessing the shark feeding scenario was my first experience, I enjoyed it and although the shark was not agressive while taking the bait, I still behold the respect for this creature's unpredictable behaviour.

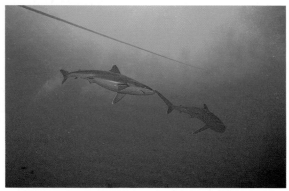

Silver tip examines the mooring line.

Air intake increases during "show time"

The leader of the pack stalks Suzanne from the back.

After a patient wait, the leader of the pack took the bait.

In two gulps the tuna disappeared into its jaws.

With a mouth full of tuna, the silver tip swims towards the cameraman.

GULF
OF
THAILAND

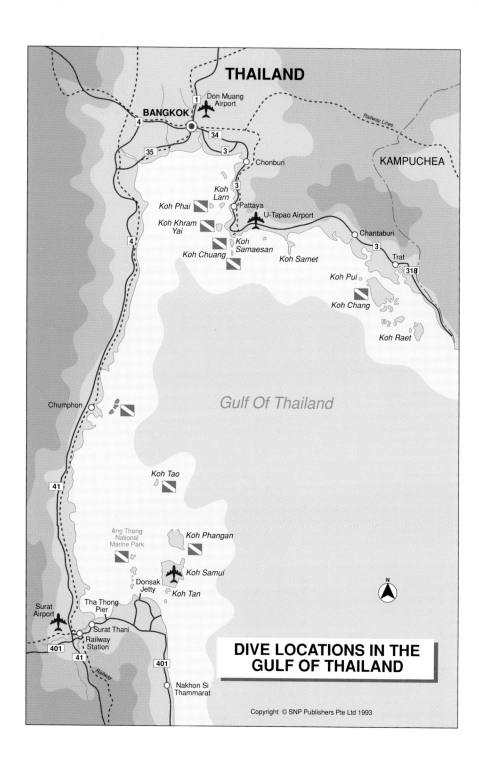

THAILAND

Don Muang
Airport

BANGKOK

KAMPUCHEA

Railway Lines

Chonburi

Koh
Larn

Koh Phai

Pattaya

U-Tapao Airport

Chantaburi

Koh Khram
Yai

Koh
Samaesan

Trat

Koh Chuang

Koh Samet

Koh Pui

Koh Chang

Koh Raet

Gulf Of Thailand

Chumphon

Koh Tao

Ang Thong
National
Marine Park

Koh Phangan

Koh Samui

Donsak
Jetty

Koh Tan

Surat
Airport

Tha Thong
Pier

Surat Thani
Railway
Station

Railway

Nakhon Si
Thammarat

**DIVE LOCATIONS IN THE
GULF OF THAILAND**

Copyright © SNP Publishers Pte Ltd 1993

THE GULF OF THAILAND

he warm waters of this sea makes diving an added pleasure, besides the alluring charms of seabed configurations from coral gardens to pinnacles, caves, "chimneys", swim-throughs and wrecks. Dive locations surrounding hundreds of islands and rocky outcrops span the Kampuchean border to the northern tip of Peninsular Malaysia.

Pattaya is the dive hub in the central and eastern seaboard of the gulf. Daily dive trips to wreck sites off *Sattahip* and *Samaesan* region are highlights conducted from Pattaya besides the inner and outer island dive programs. Live aboard dive expeditions to the archipelago of *Koh Chang* bordering Kampuchea is fast gaining popularity and there are adventurous new dive sites and wrecks to explore.

Chumphon introduces you to the abundant fish life and scenic island landmarks which are astounding with unusual natural rocky terrain. The rewards of these seascapes and landscapes have in the past, attracted mainly local divers from Bangkok. The trend is now shifting and more foreign divers are seen as land communications improve. The prime

dive sites are *Hin Lak Ngam, Koh Ngam Noi, Koh Ngam Yai and Hin Pae.*

Koh Samui offers myriad dive programs and you can choose from dive sites surrounding the *Ang Thong Marine National Park, Koh Phangan* and *Sail Rock* as full day dive program: or an overnight trip to *Koh Tao's* dive sites where big pelagic fish and awesome plankton feeders like the manta rays and the whale sharks mate and play. Staying a night in Koh Tao is like the reminiscent years of Koh Samui two decades ago.

BEST TIME TO VISIT

Pattaya's dive shops claim that the offshore dive sites are suitable the whole year round. This is a fact because there are alternative calm bays for diving at the island's dive sites, which-ever way the winds blow. Visibility is however, not always excellent through-out the year. Good visibility is experienced during the months of November to March.

Chumphon and *Koh Samui* located further south, experience some mixed weather conditions. These two dive sites are affected by the tail end of the south-west monsoon from about June to September and the tropical rain and winds of the north-east monsoon from October to late February. However, these weather factors are not continuous and there are spates of fine weather in between these periods. Records show that the months of February to May are the most favourable period for diving. In these plankton rich waters, visibility is occasionally reduced, but the profusion of fish life are rewarding sights.

DIVE LOCATIONS IN THE GULF OF THAILAND

DESTINATION	LOCATION	DIVE SITE	DEPTH	SEASCAPE & MARINE LIFE
PATTAYA	Inner Islands	Koh Larn/ Koh Sak & Koh Krok	Average 5–20m	Coral and marine life more abundant in shallow waters. Inner Islands dive sites recommended for students and new divers. Silting sometimes impair good visibility.
	Outer Islands	Koh Phai/ Koh Luam Yai/ Koh Luam Noi/ Koh Hu Chang/ Koh Klung/ Badan/ Koh Man Wichai & Koh Rin	Average 18–25m	Unusual rock formation near headlands, coral mount are sporadic on the vast sandy seabed. Strong flow of current prevails. Possible sights of sharks and eagle stingrays amongst other pelagic fish.
	Sattahip	Petchbury Bremen Wreck	22–24m	93 metres steel freighter sank in early 1930s now turned into an underwater garden. Damaged at mid section stern and bow. Prolific soft corals, sea fan and sponges. Good chance of spotting big fishes and Black Tip Reef Shark.
	Koh Samaesan	Hardeep Wreck	25–27m	Still intact after sinking in the 2nd World War by Allied Forces. Main damage in engine room. Possible careful swim through the hatches. Rich coral encrustment, sea whips place host to wing oysters, soft corals, coralline algae of black, red and violet. Murex shell and sea urchin apparent.
CHUMPHON		Hin Lak Ngam	Average 27m	Hard & soft corals grow on surface of undulating rocks. Abundant micro scopic food attracting schools of fish. Possible sighting of the whale shark and the manta ray.
		Koh Ngam Noi & Koh Ngam Yai	10–18m	Narrow swim-throughs, healthy collection of soft and hard corals. Varieties of big resident fish found under rock ledges and little caves. Scenic landscapes.
		Hin Pae	22–25m	Undulating depth, coarse sandy mount in between isolated rocks and coral heads. Mating pairs of angels and butterfly fish more apparent at depth of 10 to 18 metres.
KOH SAMUI	Koh Phangan	Koh Tae Nok & Koh Tae Nai	15–18m	Shallow dive, visibility fair. Hard and soft coral mounts, coarse sandy seabed, aquarium coral fish abundant. Long spine sea urchin community.

DESTINATION	LOCATION	DIVE SITE	DEPTH	SEASCAPE & MARINE LIFE
		Koh Mah	Average 24m	A greater part of the sloping reef are boulders in piles, forming little caves, crevices & overhanging shelter for snappers, groupers & sweetlips. Possible sightings of reef sharks, barracudas and jacks.
		Sail Rock (Hin Bai)	Average 33m	There are underwater pinnacles with gorges in between to complement wall dive pattern. Depth varies at each pinnacle and at different angles too, Soft corals more than hard corals are found here. Possible sighting of whale sharks and other big fish which migrate here to feed, mate and play.
	Ang Thong Archipelago	Koh Wao	12–18m	A rich variety of marine fish and stunning corals. There are more aquarium fish than pelagic forming healthy colonies amongst hard and soft corals.
		Hin Nippon (Jap Rock)	27–32m	Undulating outcrop with nooks and crannies inviting prolific breeding of marine crustaceans. Resident fish includes snappers, oriental & spotted sweetlips and grunters inhabiting amongst maze of rocks and swim throughs.
	Koh Tao	Ao Leuk	8-12m	Rock piling, encrusted by coralline. Neptune cups prominent. Small sea cucumber & sporadic clusters of staghorns.
		Red Rock	15–20m	Prolific fish life, abundant loose branches of gorgonian corals, sea whips, pelagic fish constantly around. Dull sea anemone communities, skunk clown fish make appearance.
		Koh Nang Yuan (Night Dive)	Average 12m	Crimson coloured gorgonian corals, vampire fish active. Zig zag oysters abundant on walls. Shrimps and small crabs study possible.
		Northern Pinnacles (Chumphon Pinnacles)	Max. 45m	A host of pelagic fish life. Spanish mackerels, tunas, queenfish, barracudas are common visitors. Occasional sighting of whale shark. Gorges and chimneys.
		Green Rock	15–18m	Submerged rock outcrops. Green turtle sighting, reef sharks, small caves homes to snappers and sweetlips.
		White Rock	18-22m	Submerged rock outcrops, prevailing current. Fish life abundant, plankton feeders and predator fish. Aggressive titan trigger.

These "silvers" symbolize prolific waters.

Brought to light seafan polyps feeding on drifting plankton.

PATTAYA

Pattaya is a city resort in the province of Chonburi on the Eastern Seaboard. It is also a popular dive base in the *Gulf of Thailand* which has attracted divers who wish to explore World War II wrecks, old coin and pottery wrecks. Its offshore islands offer equally interesting dive sites almost the whole year round in this sheltered bay.

Wreck diving in Pattaya commands a different adventure. Conversations exchanged and questions asked have always injected the excitement of chance encounters with big fish amongst the wrecks. When you are enquiring about the wrecks in some of the dive shops on the beach road, the stories told on wrecks will quite easily win you over to sign up.

Pattaya is a place for student divers, experienced divers and underwater photographers. The inner islands have comfortable shallow dive sites for beginners, the outer islands offer deeper dives for the experienced divers and the wrecks instill greater adventure.

Dive shops found in Pattaya are well equipped and are run by foreign and local competent dive instructors. Some having more than a decade experience with the surrounding waters. Schools for diving are found here and you can also advance your current certification or just enjoy scuba diving as a sport.

Clear waters and surrounding reefs on these islands have also attracted many picnickers to its shores every morning. *Koh Larn* is the most popular island and between 8.00 a.m. to 10.00 a.m., the sea between Pattaya and the islands are bustling with inboard and outboard boats, ferrying passengers for a day of swimming, snorkelling or parasailing.

Pattaya is 154 km from Bangkok and efficient transfers by land both ways have kept Pattaya busy with visitors. The U-Tapao Airport near to Pattaya occasionally receives chartered flights. A check with your travel agent for current flight operation is advisable.

IN THE BEGINNING....

One could hardly imagine that popular Pattaya was once a quiet fishing village on stilts, where simple fishing folks reaped the harvest from the sea and yarned through the night. The fame of Pattaya as a beach resort grew almost 'overnight' when the American servicemen decided to use it as a rest and recreation centre during the Vietnam war.

When the war ended, businessmen saw its potential as a beach resort for tourists. Their foresight of Bangkok as the capital gateway spurned into a rapid massive build up. Thus, Pattaya's development is different from other beach resorts. It was not discovered by back packers and did not go through the stages of development to become a sought-after holiday destination like many of the popular beach resorts in Thailand today.

PATTAYA TODAY....

Pattaya is dubbed as *Queen of Asia* for its unrivalled entertainment and attractions throughout the day. This premier beach resort in the *Gulf of Thailand* offers funfilled beach activities on its offshore islands and Pattaya's night life is also equally exciting.

As a city resort, Pattaya offers an impressive range of accommodation to suit your taste and budget. Some deluxe beach-front and cliff-top hotels are amongst the finest in Thailand that command grand views of headlands and bays.

Island discovery tours are major attractions luring a number of visitors from Pattaya every day. In the morning, the beach front is busy transferring visitors with passenger boats from inboard to the fast outboards for a day's picnic on the islands.

An excellent choice of international and Thai restaurants are never too far from one another, especially seafood restaurants. For a greater choice of the evening dining, shopping and entertainment, head down to sunset strip in South Pattaya for a combination of pleasant times.

Horse riding, go-karting, bowling, bungy jumping, archery and small arms shooting are some of the inland attractions. While catching the spills and thrills of jet-skies and skiing, remember that Pattaya is reputed for the best parasailing take-off from floating pantoons. On the way to the popular island of *Koh Larn* you will see more than a dozen parasails flying like colourful kites in the skies.

Above: Discerning divers stay at the Royal Cliff and enjoy the dive cruise on the Hanumarn Junk.

Pattaya is also a paradise for tropical fruit lovers for it is within the fruit growing zone of ChonBuri. The road to Pattaya during the festive fruit seasons is lined with fruit stalls displaying a variety of orchards' in all colours, shapes and sizes.

90

GETTING TO KNOW YOUR DIVE PROGRAMS

The best time for diving is from *November* to *March* when the waters are calm and clear, but diving goes on all year round in Pattaya. This is primarily because there are ample lees at the offshore island dive sites even during the low season when the winds are sometimes strong and tropical rain prevails.

Above: Loading of dive equipment on Pattaya Beach.

Pattaya is one of the oldest dive centres in Thailand and this sport started during the time when U.S. Armed Forces came to this beach for the R & R programs in the early 1970s.

Dive programs from *Pattaya* focused mainly on day trips to offshore island dive sites and wreck diving. Daily dive trips include, the **inner islands** of *Koh Larn, Koh Sak* and *Koh Krok*; and the **outer islands** of *Koh Phai, Koh Luam Yai, Koh Luam Noi, Koh Hu Chang, Koh Klung Badan, Koh Man Wichai* and *Koh Rin*. Dive boats set off from *Pattaya Beach* in the early morning and return to shore in the late afternoon.

Wreck diving in *Pattaya* is a highlight of this region, providing an exciting dive scenario. The *Petchbury Bremen wreck* is located off the Sattahip coast, close to *Koh Khram Yai* and *Koh Khram Noi*. The *Hardeep wreck* is off the coast of Samaesan town, in the seabed between Koh Samaesan and Koh Chuang. Structures of these wrecks remained intact, but some sections of its steel hull are corroded and others thinned out.

Both wrecks are located more than 4 hours by boat from Pattaya. Hence the shorter journey by land to the respective piers followed by transfers by dive boat to the dive sites is practical and with enough time for two dives.

Chinese junk wrecks which were carrying coins and pottery sank some 600 years ago. Remains of this wreck are some decayed timber pieces which are covered with old fish nets.

▲ *Wreck salvage from Petchbury Bremen.*

The coins were stored in jars filled to prevent discolouration and in time, the charcoal solidified on the coins. Fishermen who found the wreck, broke the jars thinking there were great treasures within. It turned out that the coins were worthless but the jars were more valuable. The heavy weight of the jars also prevented the fishermen from hauling them up. When news broke that the ancient pottery had value, it became a 'treasure' for the fishermen who found it. Dive trips to these sites include land transfers and this saves travelling time.

▲ *Studded star on branches of corals with similar characteristics.*

Above: Divers ready to take the leap off Hat Nuai.

Until now, the dive sites around *Koh Chang,* the second largest island near the Kampuchea border and its numerous smaller islands, have virtually not been explored. Dive trips there are now being initiated by *The Scuba Professional* on a live aboard program from Pattaya. It will not be too long before other dive shops add this program to the existing ones.

Sail and Dive Program
The Royal Cliff Beach Resort outdoor sports division initiates a special learn-to-dive program for its discerning guests at its swimming pool.

Guests who are interested in scuba diving are invited to free pool lessons before the open waters experience. Qualified instructors from **Seafari Sports Center** are appointed to instruct and introduce the benefits of scuba diving. After theory and pool lessons, student divers are given the option to make reservation to be on the **Hanumarn Sailing Junk** for a sail and dive program. A flash of crimson covers the authentic sails which almost reaches

the deck, making it one of the most pronounced boat in the Gulf of Thailand.

After retiring to the comforts of luxurious rooms, memories of the diving and sailing experience are kept vivid as guests are able to see the *Hanumarn Junk* moored in front of the *Royal Cliff Beach Resort.*

DIVE SHOPS
Scout along the sea front road of Pattaya Beach for the numerous dive shops. Although the shops may be located within the hotels' premises or along the side road, you are able to see their billboards by the road, on the walls or hanging from an advertising post for prominence.

Unlike the shops in Phuket that advertise dive trips in advance, those in Pattaya seldom. You can walk into any dive shop and make enquiries and the programs will be well presented. Some operate on a Monday to Sunday fixed schedule to either the inner islands, outer islands or wreck diving.

During the high season most of these trips are active with ample divers signing up. But during the low season, when there are few divers, shops liaise with each other for a possible team up of a minimum of four divers to make the dive trip viable.

A one-day dive trip is the trend and hence, all equipment is stored on shore at the shops' premises. Live aboard or overnight dive expedition from Pattaya are specially arranged trips as there are few boats designed for this program. On a day to day basis, only sufficient air tanks are carried on board together with other gear for the day's trip and are unloaded after diving.

93

DIVE BOATS

Boats chartered for dive programs are basic passenger ferry boats converted from Thai fishing boats and only some have dive platform and tank slots. However, there is a spacious front deck with benches for divers to sit. Dive equipment are usually packed in plastic oblong baskets and if there are no tank-slots, air-tanks are stacked in between benches to prevent them from rolling.

Longtail boats are used to transfer divers and equipment to the dive boats when the tide is too low for it to nose-in cautiously ashore for loading.

On a wreck dive program, taking off from a fishing pier at *Sattahip* or *Samaesan* town, fishing boats are chartered for the dive trip. Only a few fishing boats have additional benches and canvas shelter as additional facilities.

DIVE PACKAGES FROM PATTAYA

Prices in dive packages may vary according to the program, the duration, the type of dive boats and its facilities , as a general guideline:

One Day Inner Islands Dive ....1,000–1,200 baht
(2 dives inclusive of tanks & weight belt only)
One Day Outer Islands Dive ....1,000–1,400 baht
(2 dives inclusive of tanks & weight belt only)
One Day Wreck Diving ....1,800–2,000 baht
(2 dives inclusive of tanks & weight belt only)
Operators ....All dive shops

Dive Expedition Program:
Koh Chang Dive ....1,500 baht per day (Average trip 5 days)
(unlimited dives inclusive of tanks & weight belt, optional accommodation on Koh Chang)
Current Operator ....The Scuba Professionals

PATTAYA'S DIVING FRATERNITY

The Scuba Professionals
1/1 Moo 3 Pattaya Naklua Road
Tel: (038) 221860, 221861
Fax: (038) 221618
Pattaya & Eastern Seaboard

Paradise Divers
Siam Bayview Hotel
Pattaya Beach Road
Tel: (038) 423871-8,
Fax: (038) 423879

Seafari Sports Centre
359/2 Soi 5, Pattaya Beach
Tel: (038) 429060, 429253
Fax: (038) 424708

Max's Dive Shop
Nipa Lodge, Beach Road, Pattaya
Tel: (038) 428195, 428321

Reef Divers Co.
Ocean View Hotel, Beach Road
Pattaya Tel: (038) 428084, 428434

Sea and Sea
Pattaya Beach Road, Pattaya
Tel: (038) 426517

Steven's Dive Shop
Soi 4, Pattaya Beach Road, Pattaya
Tel: (038) 428392

▲ *Macro view — intricate maze pattern of brain coral.*

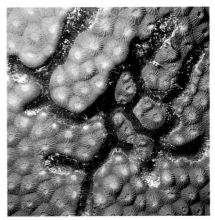

▲ *Fracturing of star corals caused by disease.*

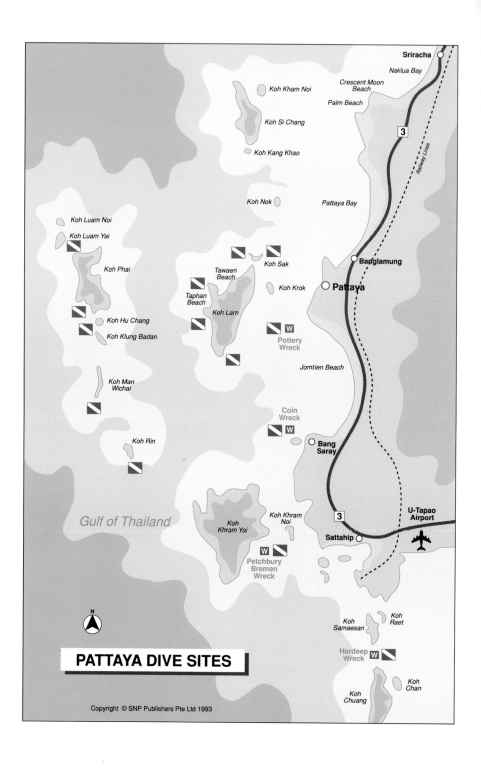

PATTAYA DIVE SITES

Copyright © SNP Publishers Pte Ltd 1993

DIVE SITES OF PATTAYA

INNER ISLANDS DIVE SITES

Travelling time to the inner island dive sites is about 45 minutes and the journey across the open sea is generally choppy as there is a constant high and low wind blowing in the gulf.

The surrounding waters off *Koh Larn, Koh Sak* and *Koh Khrok* are good dive sites frequently visited by dive operators. Of these 3 islands, *Koh Larn* is the largest with beautiful beaches and neighbouring coral reefs for diving, swimming and snorkelling.

Below: Open water students exploring the shallow reefs of Hat Neun.

Above: Koh Phai — one of the Outer Islands which is still under naval protection, but naval authority has relaxed its restrictions on some beaches.

Dive sites are located off headlands on the west, north and southern tip of the island away from where the tourist crowd gather daily. (Headland in the Thai language is referred to as *Laem*.) *Laem Tham Rae, Laem Har Nuan, Laem Thian* and *Laem Sang Wan* are some of the popular dive sites.

The first dive is usually conducted at *Koh Larn*, off one of the headlands. The second dive is conducted off the southern curved coast of *Koh Sak* or off the west coast of *Koh Khrok* for a shallow dive before heading back. Student divers are brought to these sites for their "open waters" experience.

97

Characteristics

There is evidence of corals being destroyed by fish dynamiting, but with strict supervision by marine authorities, marine life are found to be prolific in shallow waters. Juvenile staghorns, mushroom corals and sponges are apparent. The Inner Island dive site depth is between 5 to 15 metres. But at the northern tip of *Koh Larn,* the depth reaches 18–20 metres.

Dive Scenes

Past fish dynamiting have caused coral reef destruction, however there are evidence of healthy juvenile corals growing in between the coral "rumbles".

Staghorn corals border the patches of the older brain corals, pore corals and table corals; while soft corals and spiky sponges intermingle. Sea anemone and their damsel and clown fish playmates are noticed amongst less densely populated coral mounts. The small caverns and crevices of hard corals harbour families of spinefoot fish, squirrel fish and blue head damsels. The dominating black damsels darting in and out of coral heads are bigger than species in the Andaman Sea.

Sea whips and sea fans grow densely in some areas and the numerous polyps on their lengths give them a fluffy look. These fluffy polyps retract when you come too close or touch them and emerge after a few minutes. A fair quantity of sponges like the stately looking Neptune cups branch out from the base and corners of coral heads.

Visibility in a good season can reach a distance of about 8 to 10 metres but during the low tide with prevailing strong winds and currents, visibility can drop. On an average, the sites of the inner islands are suitable and satisfying for a student or novice diver.

Above: "Spot me if you can" — scorpion fish.

OUTER ISLANDS DIVE SITES

Dive trips to outer islands of *Koh Phai, Koh Luam Yai, Koh Luam Noi, Koh Hu Chang, Koh Klung Badan, Koh Man Wichai* and *Koh Rin* cost more than dive trips to the inner islands because it is located further and chartering of the boat costs more. The difference is about 15 to 20 percent more than dive programs to the inner islands.

Most of these islands are Thai Navy territories and landing is not encouraged near naval installation. However, there is a beautiful beach on the eastern coast of *Koh Phai* which is away from naval installation where boatmen bring tourists for its secluded beauty. The tourism related businesses are trying to negotiate with the Naval Authority to have more sites. Travel time to the furthest island of *Koh Rin* takes about two hours.

Characteristics

Unusual rock formations near headlands, coral mounts are sporadic on the vast sandy seabed. Strong flow of currents prevail. Possible sightings of sharks and eagle rays amongst other species of pelagic fish.

Dive Scenes

Amongst all the islands, *Koh Rin's* visibility is generally good as it is located further away from the other islands and not affected much by back wash and silting. The depth is between 18 to 20 metres with possible sightings of big pelagic mid water fish, groupers, snappers and blue spotted stingrays. Brain and boulder pore corals form mounts, mazes and swim-throughs in this reef and are natural habitats for anemones, sea urchins, feather starfish and a wide variety of parrots, butterfly, angel, file, box and wrasse fish.

After this dive, the dive boat travels on a 1½ hour journey to another exciting site at *Koh Luam Yai*. The depth here is between 18 to 25 metres and it is here that divers get to see black tip reef sharks as the main attraction. Stay close to your dive master if you feel nervous.

There are alternative dive sites from *Koh Phai* on the south western bay. This sporadic spread of coral beds with vast sandy seabeds are mating and breeding grounds for the blue crabs. Off its southern headland is the island of *Koh Hu Chang* and the channel in between has strong currents which support the excitement of drift diving towards *Koh Klung Badan.*

It is like an effortless floating sensation and the current flow will bring you through seabed scenes from coral reefs to rocky and coarse sandy sea floors. Swimming with the current gives you a great chance to see stingrays, jacks, barracudas and queenfish which are active with the flow of the current.

PETCHBURY BREMEN WRECK

The *Petchbury Bremen* met its fate in the early 1930s. How it actually sank is unknown, but if you speak to the veteran divers of this region, they say the ship sank after an explosion in the hull of mid-ship which turned into an inferno. It is believed that the 300 footer steel freighter managed to stay afloat until most of its cargoes were salvaged.

The wreck is located off the fishing village of *Sattahip* in a depth of about 23 metres. It rests upright on the sandy seabed and besides its original damage at mid-ship, sections of its bow and stern are also damaged, probably by naval exercises.

Characteristics

The sea has claimed the wreck and turned it into an artificial reef filled with marine life. It is now an underwater garden where exotic soft corals, sea fans, sponges and bivalve shells encrust the 300 feet of steel structure. Hardly a square inch remains unencrusted and its chambers and hull are now homes, playgrounds, mating and feeding venues for multitudinous creatures and plants. Encountering moray eels and resident big fish are just some of the wreck adventures. Dive depth: 22–24 metres.

Dive Scenes

It takes an experienced captain to locate the wreck in the open sea as there are no indicators other than islands and mainland bearings. When the anchor catches the wreck, divers descend by following the anchor rope. Upon ascending, a crew member or dive master checks that the anchor is not in a complicated hold for withdrawal.

Strong currents prevail in this channel; and a more comfortable dive will be during the peak or at the lowest tide when the current slacks. However, visibility is best at high tide when the awesome image of the wreck comes into your view as you descend after 12 to 15 metres. Swimming into the wreck can only be done by experienced divers and this will be explained during pre-dive sessions.

Colours of the wrecks are vivid amongst clusters of gorgonian sea fans, orangy pinkish and purple encrusting coralline algae, soft purple pink cauliflower corals and steadfast looking barrel sponges. Zig zag oysters and wing oysters grow healthily and a multiple of

Above: Fishing boats are used for Hardeep wreck dives. All dive related equipment are loaded and off loaded after each dive program.

bivalve shells wedge themselves on nooks and corners of the wreck. Sea whips with their base usually in the wreck branch out with a few wing oysters clinging onto its slender branch. In sporadic branches, the black corals are found at dark corners of the wreck. Be wary of those feathery hydroids with stinging cells and spiky urchins when you are closing in to view what's within the numerous steel frames.

The wreck encompasses the living sea as you swim on and focus on macro vision. With good visibility, scan for the active cleaner shrimp, snapping shrimp, sea slugs, worms, tiny crabs and a host of others amongst the irregular steel structure of this underwater flora on the wreck.

Sometimes there are shoals of idle yellow tail fish surrounding the wreck during slack tides and as soon as there is current, they begin feeding on the plankton. They are far more common than other fish at mid-water around the wreck. Turtles attracted by the noise of bubbles close in for a glance, huge moray pop their heads, their mean look, merely belie their placid nature. When you are doing a swim through via the deck section into the hull and out of the frame work of the wreck, look out for the big groupers and snappers which stir up silt as they bolt to safety. Divers have occasionally seen eagle rays flapping their wings gracefully when they exit from the wreck.

The second dive, after surface interval time for a light meal and rest, is conducted at *Koh Khram Noi.* The surrounding coral reefs here appear to be stunted in growth in these shallow waters of 3 to 10 metres which are constantly subjected to prevailing strong winds and big waves during the rough weather season. Black tip reef sharks are occasionally spotted here and they give divers something to be excited about and record in their dive log.

THE HARDEEP WRECK

Local fishermen of Samaesan fishing village say that the *Hardeep* was sunk by Allied Forces in the Second World War when it was cruising the deep channel between *Koh Samaesan* and *Koh Chuang.* The journey by boat from the pier takes about 35 minutes with scenic views of undulating hills, mangroves, estuary and fish farming along this waterway.

The wreck is located between the island of *Koh Samaesan* and *Koh Chuang.* Depending on the tide factor, the *Hardeep Wreck* lies between 25 to 27 metres in deep blue waters.

Above: Coral garden outgrows the Hardeep wreck. (Photo Courtesy by Pattaya Scuba Club).

Characteristics

This wreck is in a better condition than the Bremen wreck as the steel plates on most areas are still intact although some areas are corroded. You can penetrate the wreck from mid-ship and the deck area, through the steel frames.

Dive Scenes

Divers do the walk-in entry and wait at the anchor rope for instructions to begin their descend. You will not be able to see the wreck from the surface as the visibility is constantly impaired by silt and plankton from prevailing currents.

A blur vision of the wreck appears after 8 to 10 metres and you reach its deck at about 15 metres. You will spot the dive boat's anchor holding onto one of the steel frames. The dive master checks the hold of the anchor and adjusts it if necessary for an easy withdrawal.

Above: A metre from this landmark lies the Hardeep wreck at a depth of 25 metres.

It is interesting to swim around the deck area and check out the probable entry point into the wreck before descending another 10 to 12 metres to reach the seabed. Residents of the wrecks like morays, snappers and groupers are shy of divers and will remain inside the wreck. With an underwater torch light you may be able to spot these fish before they swim deeper into one of the many narrow chambers.

Swimming round the wreck is usually done before attempting to enter the wreck. Other than the concentration of marine flora and fauna on the wreck, the surroundings are just sandy with small mounts of patch corals and abandoned fish traps and some old fishing nets.

101

Encompassing the whole wreck is a dense growth of corals and algae of variable colours and shapes. There are numerous tiny cleaner wrasses, graceful butterfly and angel fish swimming and feeding on coral polyps. The bat angel fish and Moorish idols make their presence felt by darting across your path when you peer into the frame of the wreck.

Equally abundant are also sea urchins and murex shells which are found at the base of the wreck and amongst the nooks and corners of the entire framework. Feather starfish, sea fans and flowery soft corals, wing oysters and zig-zag oysters form part of the sights and colours of the *Hardeep Wreck*.

Above: *Crown-of-thorn starfish — predator of corals.*

A shallow second dive will either be conducted at *Koh Juan* or *Shark Fin Rock*. At *Koh Juan* bay, the depth of 10–15 metres introduces numerous patches of hump corals and brain corals. The Neptune cups sponges have lateral growth like extra arms. Parrot fish, sand breams, lizard fish, rabbit fish and big wrasses dominate the wreck area.

At *Shark Fin Rock*, the depth is about 18 metres and there is more marine life spreading some 20 metres around the base of the rocky structure. The numerous little caverns are homes to squirrel and rabbit fish while the black damsels prefer the shades of table corals. Its cousin, the reticulated damsel, plays hide-and-seek with divers often darting into the safety of the stumpy young antler corals.

These two sites provide a comfortable second dive before heading on back to *Samaesan* fishing village. Remember that the sun will be in your favour on the return journey, so do not miss out some of the attractive landscape sceneries.

Above: *The natural saviour of coral reefs — the triton shell which feeds on the crown-of-thorn.*

102

KOH CHANG

▲ *There are many unexplored dive sites like this surrounding the Koh Chang Archipelago which offers discovery dives.*

D iving in the waters of *Koh Chang* gives you a chance to discover uncharted sites with dive operators. Sports diving is just budding around the waters which surrounds 52 islands and islets that were deprived of rapid development for the past two decades, because of war turmoil in neighbouring Kampuchea and Vietnam. *Koh Chang*, the largest island in this archipelago is also the second largest island in Thailand.

With peace accord steadily building up in these neighbours, the islands have the potential to grow into famous beach resorts together with its diving industry. Currently Pattaya is the main take-off point to this destination.

The introduction of *Koh Chang* dive sites is based on a feasible program by *Scuba Professional* in Pattaya who has been in vast dive related operations for more than two decades.

DIVE EXPEDITION PROGRAM

Scuba Professionals conduct dive expeditions to *Koh Chang,* with the first leg of the journey by land transfer from *Pattaya* to *Sattahip Pier* where their well-designed 17 metre dive boat is moored. This 45-minute trip by land is practical because the distance by sea, will take a lengthy four hours.

The boat has built in bunks for six divers and ample space on the deck for another six with mattresses supplied. It carries 800 litres of fresh water for shower; ice chests and live bait compartments for fishing if trolling is incorporated along the way.

For entertainment, there is a video on board with underwater movies as high-lights. Equipped with a depth finder, G.P.S. Navigation System, a back up 10 KV generator, radio and an experienced captain who is also a qualified dive instructor, diving in *Koh Chang* is worth it.

The journey to *Koh Chang* takes approximately 12 hours from *Sattahip.* Diving conducted along the way include coral reefs and wreck dives near *Sattahip* and *Samaesan* waters. These enroute dive sites are a bonus if you have not done wreck diving. After two days and two nights in these waters, the boat cruises to *Koh Chang* waters where diving commences at charted and uncharted dive sites.

There is accommodation on *Koh Chang* and on some other islands. If you wish to stay on the island, please inform the dive operator when signing up for the dive program.

The attractions of pristine beaches, swaying coconut palms and a backdrop of lush tropical forested hills amidst authentic cottages by the sea are alluring.

On the sixth day, divers will be transferred to *Trat* province on the mainland, where air-conditioned mini buses take divers to Pattaya or Bangkok. This land transfer is a better idea than the long return journey by boat.

The dive boat engages on a return dive expedition back to *Sattahip* with a new group of divers from *Koh Chang.*

For more information on this dive package from Pattaya, contact *Scuba Professionals* at Tel: (038)221860, 221861 or Fax: (038) 221618 or on Koh Chang: Magic Bungalows, Coconut Beach Tel: (01) 3290408.

Best Time To Dive

Diving in *Koh Chang* can be conducted year round, however, the best visibility and calm waters are during the months of *November* to *March.* The good season creates ripples and gentle waves that do not churn the seabed and bring silt to mid waters.

DIVE SITES

Waters surrounding the inner islands does not provide good visibility

▲ *Giant clam amidst a family of corals.*

primarily because of shallow depths which averages 15 metres. Channels between two islands are also affected by constant backwash from the shores. However, the lee side waters is clearer.

The outer islands which command deeper depths of 27 to 30 metres enjoy better visibility and offer myriad attractions of pinnacles, caves and unusual protuberances and fish life. Underwater boulders are a continuation of landscapes bordering the sea and are found in stacking formations due to previous earth tremors.

Pioneering divers recorded sightings of turtles, rays, giant sweetlips, grunters, snappers and sharks; besides a host of colourful aquarium marine fish which are found close to shores. This is because these waters have not been exploited by dive operators. Hence the coral reefs and marine life are found in abundance in shallow waters too. Be wary of sea urchins which are wide spread in these waters. The slender white tip reef sharks occasionally appear out of curiosity.

Currently there are two naval ship wrecks in relatively shallow waters between 12 to 15 metres. Visibility is usually fair but deteriorates during low tide. Islanders say that there are more wrecks to uncover and this offers a challenge to adventurous divers.

CHUMPHON

Chumphon is viewed as a resort on the east coast of Thailand where the southern provinces begin and is 470 km from Bangkok. It is a popular local destination and locals often drive there with their own vehicles from Bangkok for a weekend holiday.

This province is famous for its abundant seafood from the *Gulf of Thailand* and is also one of the *"fruit basins"*. Besides these, its offshore islands offer excellent dive sites but there are more locals than foreigners.

▲ *Koh Ngam Noi — where landscapes and seascapes offer captivating scenes. Cottages on the rocks are homes of bird nest collectors. (Chumphon, Gulf of Thailand)*

Destination Chumphon can be described as "a slip through the fingers" by tourists because of the odd times the trains and tour buses arrive. The arrival times are in the late evenings or in the wee morning hours. Travel agents in Bangkok, Ranong, Phuket and Surat Thani are beginning to operate air-conditioned mini coaches that arrive in Chumphon in the afternoon but the operation is still not fully set-up currently.

TOWN SIGHTS

The small town of Chumphon with a population of close to 17,000 is a busy self contained trading centre. There are to date a few hotels and entertainment centres as the influx of tourists is only just beginning.

Jansom Chumporn Hotel is the biggest hotel which offers fine air-conditioned rooms, a good restaurant and an in-house discotheque. Between 1.00 to 5.00 am the restaurant turns into a fast music dance hall which is referred to as *"Khaotomtheque."* Boiled rice in Thai is called *khao tom* and a variety of local dishes are served here.

The *Rita Food and Drink* which is located at Chumphon Rama Theatre, is the only place in town which has country western live music. Town life quietens after 9.00 p.m.

DIVING IN CHUMPHON

The diving industry is still young in Chumphon. Day dive programs to offshore islands and rocky outcrops located one to two hours away from the coast are organized by dive shops.

In town, information on diving is available at the *Jansom Chumporn*

Hotel on *Saladaeng Road* and at *Seafari International Ltd* on *Thatapao Road.* A more comprehensive dive program is available on *Thung Wua Laen Beach* at the *Chumphon Cabana Dive Centre.* They have been in operation for more than four years.

The Chumphon Cabana Dive Centre has comfortable accommodation on the beach, a restaurant and an open air patio where divers gather for breakfast before their trips. Diving begins between 8.00 a.m. and 9.00 a.m. All the dive equipment are transported by push carts into the shallow waters and transferred into a fibreglass row boat.

Above: Chumphon dive boats are smaller but serves its purpose to the neighbouring dive sites.

Divers may also be transferred to the dive boat by row boat,but most of them prefer to wade through the waist-high water level during the low tide. Town operation differs a little. For the day's program divers meet at the dive shop and are transferred to the pier. The dive boat is moored at the pier in the river and the route out to the estuary passes fleets of fishing boats. There are fish meal factories located on the banks of the river and the strong smell of fermented fish permeates the sea breeze at certain intervals of the journey. During low tide, the river is shallow, with winding sand banks, taking only a skilful captain to steer the boat back to its mooring site.

Dive Boats

There are big and small dive boats, which are converted from fishing boats. The small dive boats which are capable of taking 6 divers measures about 10 metres and powered by 125 h.p. diesel truck engines. These boats may not have a toilet on board.

The bigger boats are better equipped with toilets and broader deck space can carry 10 to 12 divers. These boats are not used for live aboard diving and facilities are very basic. Food, drinks and bottled drinking water together with diving gear are brought on board for the dive trip. The pleasure of a fresh water shower is not available and divers only splash their face with bottled water supplied for drinking.

DIVE PACKAGES FROM CHUMPHON

Prices in dive packages may vary according to the program, but as a general guideline:

One Day Dive Program ....800–1,200 baht
(2 dives inclusive of tanks & weight belt only)
Operators ....All dive shops

CHUMPHON'S DIVING FRATERNITY

Chumphon Cabana Dive Centre
Thung Wua Laen Beach
Chumphon
Tel: (077) 501990
Accommodation & restaurant facilities

Seafari International Ltd
Thatapao Road
Chumphon

Above: When the tide is low, carting dive equipment into knee deep water becomes necessary.

DIVE SITES OF CHUMPHON

The dive sites surrounding the islands of *Koh Ngam Noi, Koh Ngam Yai* and the outcrops of *Hin Lak Ngam* and *Hin Pae* offer excellent dive sites. Divers can experience interesting variable seabed configurations from coral gardens to rock piles and caves. The main attraction which adds colour to the sea is the extravagance of fish.

Most divers will later add into their dive log their unanimous ratings of fish life. This is a plankton rich sea and the fish life proliferate at remarkable rates.

Visibility varies according to tide and weather factors. On a favourable day, the visibility can be 20 metres but at low tides it can sometimes be only 8 to 10 metres.

Hin Lak Ngam

This dive site is located 1½ hours away from *Thung Wua Laen Beach.* The landmark comprises two weather-beaten rock outcrops. Like all other outcrops,

they are roosting homes for sea birds. As the boat approaches, these birds take flight. Sensing that the boat and divers are of no threat, they calmly resettle on the rocks.

Above: A den of black spotted sweetlips.

Characteristics

The rock outcrop gradually broadens its formation to form the reef base at 27 metres. Its walls are terraced with in between structures of crevices, holes, caves and protuberances. Hard and soft corals grow on the surfaces of these undulating formations. The abundant microscopic food amongst the corals and mid waters attract schools of fish. Possible sightings of the whale shark and manta ray.

Dive Scenes

Upon descending to a depth of 10 metres, there is a large community of sea anemones spread over a flat terrace area. These are pink tip anemones which have sparse short tentacles and the mouth is visible as compared with those with long clustered tentacles.

109

Above: Squirrel fish dominate this lair.

Although large in community, the presence of the clown fish is minimum. The pink skunk clown dominate the species of fish and live in bi-lateral harmony with their host anemone. At this depth you will find multitudes of green and yellow damsels and fusilier fish with their distinct silver bodies and yellow-striped dorsals.

There are schools of large yellow tails measuring between 20 to 25 cm in size swarming around divers as they descend to deeper depths; Attracted by the air bubbles, these fish follow the divers. Their presence near the rock structures attract resident fish like snappers and groupers. Big groupers and colonies of John snappers with a dot near the caudal fin swim around looking puzzled at divers amongst the great numbers of yellow tails.

Remain still, practise the neutral buoyancy, breathe easy and the fish will swim closer to you. If there is a prevailing strong current, lie flat on the bottom and observe the profusion of fish life but do be careful of the sea urchins.

Marine animals and plant life are found more amongst rocky formations than at the base. On the seabed observe the impressive clusters of bushy black corals with different colours of fluffy polyps in hues of orange, white, yellow and light apple green. These elegant man-size bushy black corals are beautiful subjects to photograph and with a host of fish around it will make an excellent underwater portrait.

Wing oysters which grow normally on sea whips and sea fans are found setting their roots in the sand, appearing like black pads. A circumnavigation swim reveals swim throughs and small caves where bigger fish nest.

Adding to the exotic marine life colours and characteristics are butterfly fish, angel fish, indigo goat fish, reticulated black damsels mingling around sporadic pink tip staghorn corals and crusty table corals.

The sightings of whale sharks and manta rays have been recorded in these waters during the months from February to April. These plankton feeders occasionally swim near the rock structures and like to be near small fish communities. Unafraid of divers, these rare awesome creatures usually stay around the site for a few days.

110

Above: The underwater pinnacles of Hin Lak Ngam is simply amazing. Being swarmed by pelagic fish is a daily encounter, more dramatic when the current is strong. (Chumphon)

Above: The "inflorescence" of a commonly found jewel stone coral.

Koh Ngam Noi and Koh Ngam Yai

Both islands have scanty natural vegetation amidst formations of natural artistic rock structures. The little caves and crannies found here are homes to swifts. The nests they build are the special grade of birds nest which are treasured for its nutritional values and are highly prized.

Bird's nests collectors build authentic huts on these rocky structures guarding their territory with dogs as a warning against intruders. These dogs back at any strange boats or divers surfacing near the rocks and ceases after a while when they do not sense any threat.

Of these two islands, *Koh Ngam Noi* offers more attractive landscapes of huts built on different levels of rocky headlands. The best time for photography is between 2.00 to 3.00 pm when sun shines.

These two islands are about 15 minutes apart by boat and *Koh Ngam*

Noi the nearest island from *Hin Lak Ngam* is about 25 minutes away.

The dive pattern from these two sites is planned according to which way the wind blows. The dive boat will initially moor on the lee side where divers take a rest and gear up. When it is ready to dive, the boat will steer towards the exposed part of the island, allowing the divers to get into the waters and double back to moor in the calm bay. Dive masters take their bearing and guide divers through an underwater tour back to the dive boat.

Characteristics

Narrow swim throughs, healthy collection of soft and hard corals. Varieties of big resident fish found under rock ledges and little caves. Visiting fish are more apparent during the flow of the current.

Dive Scenes

Dive sites around the islands are continuations of these two islands' rocky characteristics, forming caves and

111

unusual rock formations which are homes to snappers, sweetlips, groupers, families of angels, butterfly fish and parrot, spinefoot and surgeon fish. Here again, the yellow tails, damsels and schools of lunar fusilier fish cloud the mid waters feeding at random on floating microscopic marine animals. But as soon as current ebb, the appetite of the fish ceases and you will observe a slow down in activities. The goat fish are active at this point as they feed on the sandy seabed for traces of settled down tiny marine animals by using their two feelers at the base of their mouth.

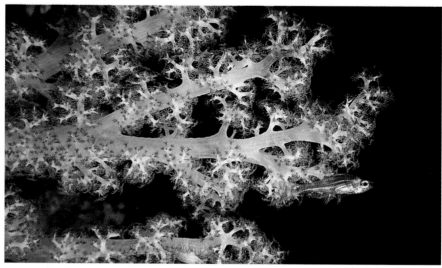

▲ *In harmony.*

The depth is very comfortable at 10 to 18 metres as you swim through the caves and gorges. Crusty table corals, staghorn corals and brain corals in individual formation grow amongst the base and corners of the rocks. Zig zag oysters, thorny oysters, wing oysters are prolific on the walls of rock terraces. Sea cucumbers and sea urchins prefer the sandy area near the edge of coral heads while the brown and white stripe feather starfish set roots on groups of sea whips and gorgonian branching corals.

These two calm dive sites are ideal mooring points for rest in between dives and also share views of scenic landscapes. The similarity of both the sites could possibly indicate that these two islands were perhaps, once linked to each other.

Visibility is about 10 metres, but the scope of fish life is viewed through a screen of micro-floating elements from plankton to smaller marine animals. Hence, the visibility may be reduced sometimes when the screen is thicker at some areas.

Hin Pae

This is the second rock outcrop dive site of Chumphon and is located at the northernmost area between these four

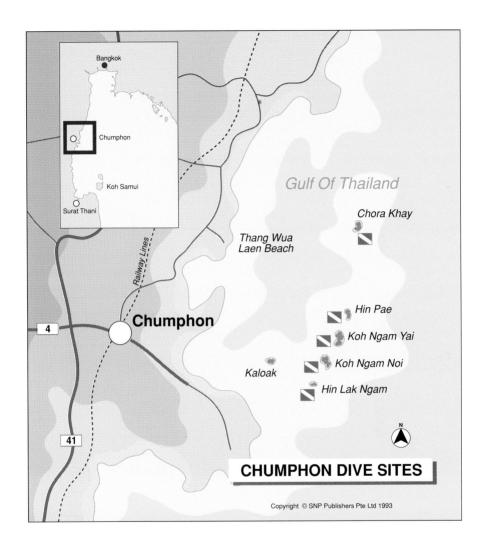

Bangkok

Chumphon

Koh Samui

Surat Thani

Gulf Of Thailand

Chora Khay

Thang Wua
Laen Beach

Railway Lines

Chumphon

4

Hin Pae

Koh Ngam Yai

Kaloak

Koh Ngam Noi

Hin Lak Ngam

41

N

CHUMPHON DIVE SITES

Copyright © SNP Publishers Pte Ltd 1993

popular dive sites of Chumphon. Travel time between *Koh Ngam Yai* and *Hin Pae* is about 20 minutes.

Characteristics
Undulating depths, coarse sandy mounts in between isolated rocks and coral heads. Mating pairs of angel and butterfly fish more apparent at depths of 10 to 18 metres. Maximum depth variable between 22 to 25 metres.

Dive Scenes
These barnacles encrusted rocky outcrop extends broadly to the seabed and at its deepest end, there are big snappers and groupers living in holes and caves. If you swim slowly, the big fish will swim out of their lairs to take a look. If there are more than four divers, it is wise to split the group into two, swim around the base from different

113

directions to increase your chance of seeing the big fish.

There are four swim throughs and some overhanging rock formations. More marine life and corals are found on the eastern side. The exotic coral fishes seen here are blue ring angels, emperor angels, Moorish idol angels and a host of butterfly fish. The lyretail wrasse are amongst the boulder fish which will swim close to divers and the porcupine puffer fish curiously trails by. Small file fish, spinefoot fish, the wandering parrots and surgeons fish are other common fish at this dive site.

The rock surfaces is covered with coralline algae, growth of sea whips and sponges. The colonies of hard corals include the independent mushroom corals in oval and round shapes, pore corals in boulder forms are embedded with bivalve shells, brain coral and its base act as the growth point for staghorn corals and the star-studded corals. On a favourable day visibility extends to 20 metres but reduces during low tide when current slacks.

If you remain buoyant close to the nooks, crannies and protuberances and you will be surprised at the existence of another interesting tiny world of shrimps and crabs.

KOH SAMUI

oh Samui with a land area of 247 sq. km is the third largest island in the Kingdom. It is under the province of *Surat Thani* and is the mainland's pride tourist attraction.

The island is the dive base and take-off point to popular dive locations in the southern regions in the Gulf of Thailand. There are diving schools along the beach for beginners and the surrounding calm waters with gradual depths has proven to be ideal for students who are on introductory diving course.

Koh Samui, Koh Phangan and the *Ang Thong National Marine Park Archipelago* offer great snorkelling sights amongst its west coast reefs. However, popular dive sites which have been charted and regularly visited by divers are located amongst the surrounding waters of islands and rock outcrops situated further north.

Dive sites at *Sail Rock* and those surrounding *Koh Tao* are rated as some of the best in the region. Dive trips to these sites require a full day or an overnight program where accommodation is arranged on the island. Live aboard diving is not the common dive pattern from *Koh Samui*.

For divers who have adored the marine fauna and flora in *Koh Samui*, are often greeted by the pervading greens and flowering shrubs of landscapes. Adding to these are waterfalls, padi fields, scenic headlands of natural rock sculptures and pervading lush tropical forests.

Air and sea links to *Koh Samui* are efficient and getting there is no problem. There is a direct service from Bangkok and Phuket operated by *Bangkok Airways*. *Thai Airways International* flies to Surat Thani on the mainland from Bangkok and Phuket too. From here, there is a fleet of fast ferries, vehicle ferries and slow evening ferries to the island at variable times.

REMINISCENT YEARS....

Koh Samui was discovered by backpackers about 1½ decades ago and they were captivated by the island's natural beauty. The pervading coconut palms which extends its elegant curves over the waterlines of dazzling white beaches were just a touch of the island's charm. As swinging hammocks were tied between the trunks of coconut palms, little cottages of differing designs were built alongside. Quaint thatched-roof food stalls appeared adjacent and that was the highlight for the early visitors.

A roof for the night cost between 30 to 60 baht, depending on the size. The evening became romantic by candle lights as there was no electric supply at the time. You could easily live in this paradise island on 100 baht a day including meals.

Above: If harassed, sea cucumber emits sticky white substance.

The good news spread and increased the number of backpackers which spurred the development of more cottages. The island took its natural course and more facilities were made available. Standard of living increased, better accommodation became apparent as different class of visitors came to the island from the mainland.

Although the island now has some of the finest beach hotels with standards comparable to Phuket and Pattaya, there are still little corners of the old days with cottages costing 150–200 baht.

Fewer backpackers now visit the island as there is fewer budget accommodation.

Above: Puffer's unique nostril.

KOH SAMUI TODAY....

In spite of its rapid growth into a popular beach resort, *Koh Samui* today can still offer the serenity of uncluttered beaches and lush tropical greens from the beaches to its hinterland. This image, is in fact the pride of the Samui people and many visitors have dubbed it the perfect tropical hideaway holiday destination. The policy of all hotels on Koh Samui is to plant abundant flowering shrubs and trees to complement the beautiful beaches. Most of them provide in-house facilities ranging from swimming pools to sporting activites. Koh Samui's ring road of 50 km only, enables you to complete the island tour and visit its hinterland attractions in a day. This narrow cement ring road is not safe for motorcycling especially in the evening as the road lights are poorly lit.

Above: "Save us from extinction".

KOH PHANGAN

The development of Koh Samui influenced the rapid progress of Koh Phangan as a tourist resort. From 70 authentic huts by the sea in 1983, the island now has 161 beach hotels with a total of 2,555 rooms.

It takes only 45 minutes by boat transfer from Koh Samui to Koh Phangan operating 2 daily services. An exchange of tourists is now felt, but Koh Samui with its airport and more frequent sea links still retains the bulk of tourists. There are also direct sea links to mainland Surat Thani and Koh Tao in the north.

On the island, boat taxis are important means of transfers to other beaches as land routes are hampered by hilly terrain.

Coral reefs are found off the beaches, however, some areas are better than others. There are smaller islands with better reefs and clearer waters for diving. *Koh Mah* is rated by divers as the best site and *Koh Tae Nok* and *Koh*

Tae Nai follow respectively. Dive shops are found on *Haad Rin Nai Beach.*

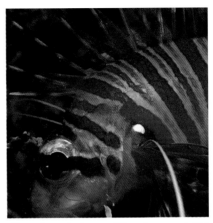

Above: Deceptive beauty of the poisonous scorpion fish.

Every month on the full moon day, *Koh Phangan's Haad Rin East Beach* attracts an influx of tourists. It is now a trend that on full moon day, all resorts organize open air parties on the beach which lasts till morning. The swing of the party begins in the evening till morning when all party goers happy and drowsy, board their pre-arranged boats back to their respective resorts.

KOH TAO

Since all the best dive sites are located near this island in this region, Koh Tao has the potential to be the next dive destination after Koh Samui. It may take two years or more, but the island sees a steady growth in this sport of scuba diving.

The island is located about four hours by boat from Koh Phangan and about five hours from Koh Samui. It is also connected to Chumphon province by boat via a 5-hour boat journey.

117

This unspoilt island has now 540 rooms and most of the accommodation here are by the beach and have only basic amenities. Lighting in some areas are by candle lights or kerosene wicker lamps. The better accommodation have electricity supplied through generators in the evening till midnight when occupancy is low. When the occupancy is high, electricity is available day and night.

Koh Tao Cottage Resort on *Ao Chaolok Kao Beach* on the southern tip has fan rooms, a restaurant on the hill, a good supply of fresh water and a scenic view of the sea. By far, this resort is the best on Koh Tao. It supplies regular transportation to the island's pier town on *Mae Haad Beach*.

The island is isolated but mobile phones are available at post offices and at Koh Tao Cottage Resort.

Mae Haad Beach is the landing point for all boat transfers from other islands and mainland. The town is also situated on this beach front and there are about 30 shop houses by the pier. There are more sundry shops than others, as they serve the needs of residents and visitors. Scuba Diving signs are obviously staked on the beach and in front of the six dive shops. Dive operators who have set up in Koh Tao realize the potential of this island. Inland routes connecting the accommodation set-ups, are mere tracks through coconut plantations and the ride on four-wheel drive pick-up trucks can be quite bumpy and over-packed at times.

ANG THONG NATIONAL MARINE PARK

The archipelago of this marine park comprises 40 islands and islets and are located about 30 km north west of Koh Samui. Daily tours take tourists for a full day picnic cruise, including snorkelling amongst its coral reefs. The name of this marine park in Thai means "golden basin".

The waters are not deep and the flow of currents in between islands cause silting and hence, visibility is average. The northern islands' deeper waters which are not affected by the silt rift offer fair dive sites whereas the inner islands are excellent for snorkelling. Dive operators do not particularly favour this dive site.

A school of sparkling fry.

GETTING TO KNOW YOUR DIVE PROGRAMS

T here are three main dive programs conducted by dive shops. They are nearby dive sites for students at *Koh Phangan*. Further dive sites at *Hin Bai* or *Sail Rock* which require 4½ to 5 hours return journey and the 2 days and 1 night dive trip to *Koh Tao* for visiting divers.

BEGINNER'S PROGRAM

Dive students who are experiencing open waters scuba diving for the first time, are taken to nearby shallow reefs where less time is spent on travelling and more time on practical lessons. They may join other divers for deeper dives after they have gained their open waters diving experience.

FULL DAY DIVE PROGRAM

The full day dive program to *Hin Bai*, a rock outcrop which appears like a sail is popularly promoted by dive shops. *"Hin"* in Thai means *"rock"* and *"Bai"* in Thai means *"sail"* and hence often referred to as Sail Rock by visitors.

All divers rendezvous at the dive shop by 8.00 a.m., check their personal dive gears and await transfer to the dive boat. It takes about three hours to reach *Hin Bai*.

Above: Koh Samui International Diving School on Chaweng Beach.

Divers assemble their air-tanks with their personal diving gears before the boat takes off. This is to enable a smooth jump off from the dive boat.

After the first dive, divers detach the B/C and regulator from the used tank and assemble them on another full air-tank and slot it into the rack for the next dive. This is practical as it will ensure minimum congestion on the deck when divers prepare to jump off. There will be ample space on the deck when divers are assembling their gears because not all divers ascend at the same time.

Other dive sites on a full-day program are *Koh Tae Nai, Koh Tae Nok, Koh Mah* near *Koh Phangan, Koh Wao* and *Hin Nippon* at the *Ang Thong Archipelago*.

OVERNIGHT DIVE PROGRAM TO KOH TAO

The overnight dive trip to Koh Tao is an exciting dive expedition if you have the time. There are ample dive sites to choose from, depending on prevailing winds and the decisions made by the dive master.

Above: "Shelter" on the rocks — Koh Tao.

Although the two way journey takes 10 hours, the encounters with the underwater world is remarkable. The profusion of fish life, submerged pinnacles, "chimneys", swim throughs and overhanging cliffs will instill the satisfaction for a complete dive holiday.

On this dive program, you can do at least four day dives, one night dive and if time and weather permits, another dive on the way back to Koh Samui. Diving is conducted at dive sites of

Red Rock; Green Rock; White Rock; Northern Pinnacle; Ao Leuk and off Koh Nang Yuan.

The **Koh Samui International Diving School** on Chaweng Beach runs regular trips to *Koh Tao* with their own boats. Pre-scheduled dates of departure are marked clearly on their beach board on display. You can sign on for the trip right on the beach.

On the day of departure, all divers meet at 8.00 a.m. and are transferred to the dive boats by inflatable dinghies and take-off at 9.00 a.m. On board, chances are you will meet divers from all walks of life so that allows you to exchange diving and cultural notes.

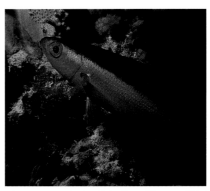

Above: An unidentified fish, almost like an artificial lure.

The journey is going to take 5 hours, so there is ample time to relax and catch that brilliant tan. A free flow of coffee, soft drinks and a basket full of bananas and oranges are supplied before your first dive. Ao Leuk is introduced as the first chosen dive site between 10 to 12 metres in a calm bay for the divers to relax after the journey.

This gives a chance for divers to climatize and adjust themselves to the changing environment. Hunger pangs grip after the first dive and a delicious meal of vegetable, chicken and rice is served. The second dive is at a depth of not more than 20 metres. After this dive, you can rest for two hours on the island before the night dive off Koh Nang Yuan.

After the night dive, a transport awaits at the pier to take divers to their accommodation for the night. The ride will be a little bumpy as uneven trails through coconut plantations are the only route of getting around.

Breakfast is served at 7.30 a.m. and you will be down by the pier at 8.30 a.m. The dive boat takes off at 9.00 a.m. for a deeper dive site. The second dive will be shallower, between 10 to 18 metres. Upon surfacing from your second dive, the boat heads back to Koh Samui. If the weather is favourable, another dive will be conducted at one of the popular dive sites closer to base — Koh Samui.

You will arrive on Chaweng Beach at twilight.

DIVE SHOPS

Dive shops/schools are found on the more popular beaches like *Chaweng Beach, Lamai Beach* and the *Big Buddha Beach.* Some have booking offices in town near the *Nathon Pier.* But you will not be able to get details on dive programs or dive courses, as dive personnel are usually stationed at the dive shops on the beach. *Chaweng Beach* has six dive shops, *Lamai* and *Big Buddha Beach* currently have one each. This is because, Chaweng Beach has the best stretch of white sandy shoreline and was the first to have been developed in Koh Samui. Hence, more dive shops and diving schools are situated here, catering for the bulk of visitors.

Above: Almost like a mermaid.

The *Koh Samui International Diving School* started in 1984 and till date, has established other branches in neighbouring islands of *Koh Phangan* and *Koh Tao.* They conduct comprehensive dive courses, well stocked with dive related equipment and boats and is one of the *Padi Dive Centers* in Thailand.

With their own dive boats, they are able to conduct more trips to further locations, with a greater choice of dive sites along the way to explore. Dive shops which do not have their own dive boats have to rely on transfer boats to the destination and from there, hire a local fishing boat to conduct the dives.

A weekly dive schedule is advertised on the beach front and you can choose your preference. The dive personnel are able to converse in English, European languages and Thai.

For a touch of local dive operators, try *Chang Diving School* which offers dive trips and conducts diving courses too.

DIVE BOATS

Dive boats in Koh Samui are converted from Thai fishing boats and are renovated to suit the dive programs. They do not have sleeping cabins or bunks like those operating in the Andaman Sea which cater for live aboard dive expeditions.

They are well designed with tank slots, air compressor on board, a common compartment for dive bags and spacious fore deck space for divers to gear up.

Live aboard diving is not the style and thus cooked food and drinks are brought on board for the day. Ample drinking water and soft drinks are supplied, but fresh water for shower is not available.

On an overnight dive trip, divers are given accommodation on the nearest island. To experience the best dive sites from Koh Samui, sign up for the *overnight dive program* to Koh Tao.

Dive boats vary in sizes and those 20 metres in length with 280 h.p. inboard diesel engines ply further distances and are capable of accommodating 16–18 divers. Smaller dive boats ply coastal waters and carry between 6–10 divers.

DIVE PACKAGES FROM KOH SAMUI

Prices in dive packages may vary according to the program, the duration, the type of dive boats and its facilities. As a general guideline:

Beginners Program:
Within Koh Samui reef ....1,200–1,400 baht
(2 dives inclusive of tanks & weight belt only)

Full Day Dive Program:
Koh Phangan
Koh Tae Nai/Koh Tae Nok ....1,500–1,600 baht
(2 dives inclusive of tanks & weight belt only)
Sail Rock (Hin Bai) ....1,600–1,800 baht
(2 dives inclusive of tanks & weight belt only)

Ang Thong National Marine Park
Koh Wao/Hin Nippon ....1,700–1,800 baht
(2 dives inclusive of tanks & weight belt only)

Overnight Dive Program:
Koh Tao (2 Day 1 Night) ....3,500–3,700 baht
(5 dives, inclusive accommodation on Koh Tao, tanks & weight belt)
Operators ....All dive shops

KOH SAMUI'S DIVING FRATERNITY

KOH SAMUI

Koh Samui Divers
Chaweng Beach
Koh Samui
Tel: (077) 421465

Chang Diving School
Chaweng Beach
Kohk Samui

Matlang Diving
Chaweng Beach
Koh Samui
Tel/Fax: (077) 421171

Calypso Diving
Chaweng Beach
Koh Samui

Pro Divers
Lamai Beach
Koh Samui

Swiss Diving Centre
Big Buddha Beach
Koh Samui

KOH PHANGAN

Koh Phangan Divers
Haad Rin Nai Beach
Koh Phangan

KOH TAO

The Scuba Professionals
Koh Tao

Koh Tao Divers
Mae Haad Beach
Koh Tao

Ban's Diving Centre
Mae Haad Beach
Koh Tao

Big Blue Divers
Mae Haad Beach
Koh Tao

Caraboa Divers
Koh Tao

Easy Divers
Koh Tao

Nang Yuan Divers
Koh Tao

DIVE SITES OF KOH SAMUI

K oh Samui is currently the main take off point inspite of the long hours across the sea to popular dive sites which are closer to other islands. This is because *Koh Samui* has the infrastructure and is one of the popular beach resorts of Thailand that receives the bulk of visitors via sea and air transfers. The other islands with less facilities to pamper visitors, are attracting more budget travellers who are not particularly drawn by scuba diving. Thus, the majority of diving enthusiasts are from *Koh Samui.*

FULL DAY DIVE PROGRAMS

Koh Tae Nok and Koh Tae Nai

These two small islets close to each other are located off the *Thongsala Pier* of *Koh Phangan.* It takes about 45 minutes by boat to reach this destination. In the Thai language, *Nok* means outer and *Nai* means inner. You either go with a dive boat or be transferred by a passenger boat to the pier and thereafter onto a local based dive boat for your dives.

Characteristics

Coral reefs are found on the northern and southern ends of *Koh Tae Nai* and at *Koh Tae Nok* the coral reefs are located at the northern bay. The outer island of *Koh Tae Nok* dive site enjoys better visibility with a greater variety of marine life. The depth varies from 15 to 18 metres and offers safe diving for beginners. Maximum visibility is about 8 metres on a favourable day when currents and silting do not occur.

Dive Scenes

Hard and soft coral mounts are sporadic with sandy seabed in between. Neptune cup sponges, pore and knob corals, star corals webbed in close growth form homes to families of fish and small crustaceans. Long spine and short spine sea urchins and sea cucumbers are found more in numbers near the sponges. Yellow tail and rabbit fish swim around in shoals while wrasses, damsels and cardinal fish prefer the crevices. Lizard and goby fish found more on the sandy seabed are hard to see until they dart off, leaving a trail of cloudy water. Beginners on this shallow dive will enjoy the maximum dive time when their air pressure gauge reads the 500 psi mark.

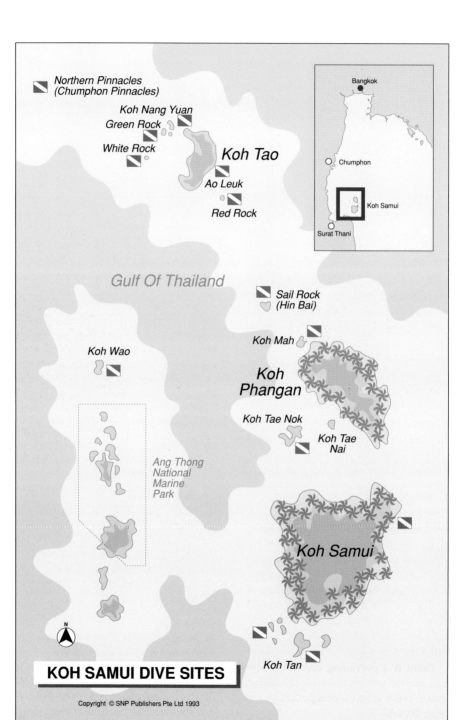

Northern Pinnacles
(Chumphon Pinnacles)

Koh Nang Yuan

Green Rock

White Rock

Koh Tao

Ao Leuk

Red Rock

Bangkok

Chumphon

Koh Samui

Surat Thani

Gulf Of Thailand

Sail Rock
(Hin Bai)

Koh Mah

Koh Wao

Koh
Phangan

Koh Tae Nok

Koh Tae
Nai

Ang Thong
National
Marine
Park

Koh Samui

N

Koh Tan

KOH SAMUI DIVE SITES

▲ *The manta ray soars. (Photo courtesy by Mark Strickland)*

Koh Mah

This dive site is located off the north western coast of *Koh Phangan.* It takes about 1½ hours from *Koh Samui* by dive boat. On this full day dive program, divers will be given time to relax on one of the popular beaches on *Koh Phangan* during the rest time before the second dive. This will give divers a chance to get acquainted with the local settings and lifestyle.

There is a prevailing current at this dive site off the west coast of *Koh Mah* hence, there is more pelagic fish swimming around.

Characteristics

A greater part of the sloping reef are boulders in piles, forming little caves, crevices and overhanging shelters for resident fish like snappers, groupers and sweetlips. Maximum depth is about 24 metres and the seabed is a continuation of the rocky headland.

Dive Scenes

Engulfing coralline algaes cover the rock surfaces, soft sponges grow from nooks and crannies. Anemone corals and stubby staghorn corals with mounts of pore corals are more apparent on the deeper ends. Lengthy sea whips with fluffy polyps in full bloom trapping micro marine food grow from the base of boulders.

Visibility reaches 10 to 15 metres and if you remain stationary periodically, the shy reef sharks are likely to appear and steal glances. Small goggle eyed groupers with light brown and pink stripes are abundant. They are indifferent to divers and you can almost touch them. Do be careful of the sea urchins, especially the small ones that embed themselves in little cave-ins of coral heads.

Pelagic fish like barracudas, garfish, queen fish and trevally make their appearance when the current is stronger to feed on fish fry which stray from overhangs and crevices.

Most of the time, you will be seeing things at eye level, but try occasionally to look up and catch the silhouettes of mid water predator fish in pursuit of their prey. The garfish and barracuda stay close to the water surface and with a burst of speed, chase their preys, often leaping out of the waters in hot pursuit.

Sail Rock (Hin Bai)

This round shape rock outcrop which rises dramatically from a depth of 33 metres and breaks the water level to soar 50 feet high, is one of the popular full day program dive sites of Koh Samui for advance divers.

Located 2 hours 40 minutes from Chaweng Beach, the dive trip begins early at 8.30 a.m. for two dives.

Characteristics

There are 12 underwater pinnacles with gorges in between to complement a wall dive pattern. The depth varies at each pinnacle and at different angles too.

More soft corals than hard corals are found here. Possible sightings of whale sharks and other big fish which migrate here to feed, mate and play.

Dive Scenes

The rock outcrop does not broaden dramatically to the seabed but offer drop-offs at some areas. There are 12 submerged pinnacles to explore in this dive site. Breathing gets a little heavy and rapid initially upon the descend as you familarize yourself on your first encounter with this maze of unusual seabed configurations.

Above: A seasonal encounter of alabaster sea cucumbers on the walls of a Neptune cup.

Surrounding you on your way down will be a school of fish like black banded barracudas, yellow tails and schools of fish fry darting in dense groups like moving shadows.

There are bushes of black corals between crevices and some grow from rock structures. Lesser hard corals are seen here, more of the soft coral species are noted. Bigger fish like the groupers and snappers are found in mating pairs and so are the other pelagic fish. This dive site is an obvious mating and spawning rendezvous for families of fish.

Lone whale shark often swim close to the surface to feed on dense plankton. Unperturbed by divers it sometimes stays for a few days before swimming away.

For a more adventurous dive to spot grey reef sharks, swim away from the pinnacles and descend to a depth between 37 to 40 metres. The seabed and its surroundings are less colourful and have large communities of sand anemones. Found amongst the small mounts of rocks are metre long spotted moray eels.

Koh Wao

This dive site is located about two hours by boat from Koh Samui. Being one of the northernmost islands of the *Ang Thong Archipelago*, the waters are relatively clear.

Characteristics

The depth ranges from 12 to 18 metres. A wealth of coral display with dense population of small coral fish and less pelagic fish. The visibility ranges from 10 to 20 metres but increases on a favourable day.

Dive Scenes

Coral life here is rich in colours as it receives sufficient sunlight through shallow waters.

As you step off from the dive boat, your body impact in the waters will send a momentary shock wave and the green damsels usually swim in shoals above coral heads and disperse frantically but reunite once you are in neutral buoy-

ancy. Other species of fish from angels, butterflies and snappers take a longer time to reappear from their hidings.

Pore corals are seen in mounts with Christmas tree worms and bivalves embedded on their fractured surfaces. The neighbouring antler corals play host to black damsels and sea anemone on coral heads are never alone, the common skunk clown fish are perpetually weaving in and out of its tentacles. The brain corals form the base for feather starfish while its walls are studded with zig zag oysters.

Jap Rock (Hin Nippon)

Just ten minutes from *Koh Wao* is this rock outcrop which offers deeper dives for season divers. There is a prevailing current in these waters and the force can instil a drift dive.

Characteristics

The descending characteristics of this outcrop are undulating and its nooks and crannies invite prolific breeding of marine crustaceans. Circling at mid-waters are shoals of barracudas, yellow tails and garfish. The depth descends to 27 metres before sloping to a greater depth of 32 metres at some areas.

Dive Scenes

In the wake of strong currents, big fish species visit this site. This phenomenon happens in most open water dive sites and occasionally, the whale shark can be spotted when plankton accumulates densely near the rock outcrop.

During slack tide, the easy descend at some steep walls is enjoyable, but the pelagic fish tends to be less. But once

Above: Ghost crab under cover.

you are near the base of overhanging and jutting rocks peer into the holes and little interconnecting caves and catch glimpses of red snappers and sweetlips darting away at first sight. Focus your eyes on the openings and breathe easy and these fish will reappear curiously. You can practise this peering habit along the way and discover lairs harbouring big resident fish.

OVERNIGHT DIVE PROGRAM TO KOH TAO

Ao Leuk

This dive site is located within a calm bay on the eastern side of *Koh Tao*, closer to the southern end. Its shallow depth of 8 to 12 metres provides an excellent site for divers to climatize after a long journey from Koh Samui.

Characteristics

The seabed configuration is a continuation of the rocky coastline and piles of rocks in unusual formation encrusted with coral life can be seen. Visibility is only about 10 to 15 metres as suspended particles stay in mid water, brought about by current and waves.

Dive Scenes

At the 8 metres depth, the seabed is sandy with isolated coral mounts. Growing on the rocky base are healthy growth of sponges and sea whips. The soft orange base engulfing the coral, thrives well on the rock surfaces with patches of purple coralline algae spreading on the vacant areas. The Neptune cups are prominent amongst the sponges and its walls are covered with juvenile alabaster cucumbers. Small mounts of staghorn corals play host to schools of small white spotted damsel fish.

Strange rows of low sandy mounts built by crustaceans or fish are seen away from the coral reef. A light film of green fluffy algae cover the surface and disperse readily at the slightest wave of the palm.

Red Rock

The landmark for this dive site consists of two impressive rock outcrops jutting out of the sea; its surface is weather beaten, with natural pot holes, curves and crevices.

Characteristics

These two rock outcrops are like the tip of an ice-berg as it broadens its base to form the impressive dive sites in terraces. The gradual sloping from the surface reaches variable depths of 15 to 20 metres. A host of marine flora and fauna await divers at this site as the rock surfaces beneath the sea are encrusted with rich coral life, homes to familes of marine life.

Dive Scenes

Amongst the coral garden, the gorgonian coral with loose branches grow healthily amongst other boulder corals. Their differing orangy colour tones make them outstanding. Sea whips are found to have spiral tips and this differs with most sea whips sighted in this region. A natural phenomenon must have caused this characteristic. Their white flowery polyps give the sea whip a soft look which belie their rigidness. Boulder pore corals, star corals, staghorn corals and soft anemone corals are some of the families of this underwater garden.

Sea anemones found here appear dull with little movements from their wide spread tentacles. Seen amongst them are pink skunk clown fish. Other species of anemone fish are rare in these waters. Green, yellow tail, and reticulated damsels add colour and character to this reef as they weave amongst the maze of short staghorn corals. Triggers, spinefoot, surgeons and the Moorish idol are some of the fish actively swimming around. The dormant resident fish found here are groupers, snappers, blue spotted stingrays, moon wrasse and squirrel fish. Zig zag oysters grow on coral walls and wing oysters attach themselves to sea fans, sea whips or at times crevices of coral heads.

Visiting shoals of yellow tails light up the surrounding as they advance against the flow of current and feed on microscopic animals. Barracudas, queenfish, garfish and schools of horse mackerels visit this site to feed on the prolific fish fry population.

Visibility is about 20 metres and on a good day may reach up to 25 metres. This largely depends on the tide and the prevailing weather. Days when the water is clearer, the visiting pelagic fish are less. On such days, the plankton and microscopic animals are less in the water to attract smaller fish to feed and thus do not attract other pelagic predator fish.

Koh Nang Yuan (Night Dive)

Koh Nang Yuan comprises two islets and a mass of rock structure, These three landmarks are connected to each other by narrow strips of white sand banks and the natural divisions have formed three bays. This dive site is located 25 minutes away by boat from Koh Tao.

Night Diving

The sheltered inner bay on the eastern side offer an excellent site for night dives. Here the underwater current is at its minimum and the base of the rock structures indicate the reef perimeter in the night. These favourable factors, give divers a good dive without having to worry about straying away nor having to work against strong currents.

Above: A glory of rainbow colours.

Characteristics
Maximum depth is about 12 metres and the growth of coral life with brilliant colours are at its best.

Dive Scenes
Once you are in the waters, descend and swim towards the rocky base. Your vision narrows to where the torch light shines and the sighting of marine life are always unexpected surprises. Only nocturnal fish and crustaceans react actively to the light, whereas, the others are sleeping. The small bronze coloured vampire fish with big eyes which are normally found in coral caves and crevices in the day, now leave their lairs and swim around. Crabs and shrimps scramble into little holes as you shine your torchlight on them. One of the most impressive colours of this area is the brilliant crimson sea fans which are found by the bunches on the walls of

rocks. Zig zag oysters come in abundance and set roots on the terraces of reefs accompanied by lesser wing oysters.

Above: A star is born in the inner space of the deep blue.

Wave your torchlight on a dark night and watch the plankton illuminate like stars. It is also a nice experience to stay still and cover the torchlight with your palm when the moon is shining bright. A sense of inner space is felt greater this way when you do a night dive. Although breathing may be a little heavier on night diving, the comfortable depth of 12 metres will alllow ample time to explore marine life in the night at this site.

Northern (Chumphon) Pinnacles

There is no landmark to indicate this dive site and an experienced boat captain steers to the correct bearing by observing yonder landmarks on the islands. It is located about 40 minutes from *Koh Tao* and it was introduced to divers some 5 years ago by local fishermen.

Characteristics

The adventure this site offers are; encounters with man-sized groupers, eagle rays, barracudas, Spanish mackerels and the occasional sighting of whale sharks. There are several swim throughs amongst gorges but a cave at 25 metres that leads to an up thrust vent opening at 18 metres which is spacious for a diver to swim through, is one of the highlights of this dive site. Divers from Koh Samui describe this experience as a "chimney" excitement.

The maximum depth reaches 45 metres and the biggest pinnacle rock tapers 16 metres to the surface, with 3 smaller ones near it.

Dive Scenes

Large resident groupers are attraction at this sites and they often stray away from their lairs. A big group of divers will scare these fish. Divers swimming in pairs have a better chance of encountering these creatures. The brownish greasy grouper are less afraid of divers, but another species with light grey body and bold black stripes tend to be shy and keep their distance. A view from the top shows that this grouper has a rather big head and a small tapering body.

The barracudas are curious creatures and often freeze its motion, agape its mouth, roll its eyes for a few seconds before languidly swimming slowly away. Repeated sightings are common, as these fish follow divers and occasionally re-approach divers at close quarters.

Other pelagic fish found in this location are queenfish, jacks, trevally and tunas. Plankton eating yellow tails swim the area when the tide is on the move.

Above: This odd shape sea squirt attracted the photographer.

Other attractions at this site are mounts of sea anemone spread thickly over the rock surfaces between 16 to 18 metre depth. Swimming in and out of these sea anemone tentacles are the pink skunk clown fish with a distinct white band across their gills. The community of sea anemone appears sluggish when compared to those found in the Andaman Sea. Neptune's cup sponges are abundant and their outer walls are crawling with soft light grey small alabaster sea cucumbers.

Swaying with the current are branches of sea fans and abundant sea whips with extensive lengths of more than three metres that grow close to each other in rows.

135

Chances of divers sighting the big resident fish are always good, however, other visiting fish vary with prevailing weather, tide and moon factors. Hence, some divers report seeing a sea full of fish and sometimes at the same dive site, the volume of fish dwindle.

Green Rock (Shark Site)

This dive site is located off the west coast of *Koh Nang Yuan* which is a 25 minute boat ride from **Koh Tao**. In trying to link this dive site with its name, there are definitely no green rocks around. But the closest possible reason why it is called *Green Rock* is because of the green-back turtle in this area by pioneering divers.

Characteristics

Pile of boulders form unusual undersea architecture with swim throughs. Depth between 15 to 18 metres holds good sightings of marine life while deeper ends are coarse sandy seabed. Visibility is fair and span about 10 to 15 metres.

These swim throughs are large enough for a diver to make the exit to the other opening slowly. coral growth on the boulders are minimum and this makes the place appear barren. The excitement of this site is found in caves and tapered overhanging boulders where big fish like John snapper and grey sweetlips rendezvous.

▲ *A slumbering nurse shark.*

Dive Scenes

When all surrounding seem short of big fish, peer into these fish holes and you will find yourself face to face with these fish. The magnification from your mask will project the fish to be 30 percent bigger and this will instill some excitement.

At the first sighting, the fish may dart in frantic in their enclosed perimeter within their homes. But when you hold your breath and breathe slowly, the fish will soon learn that you mean no harm and they will become curious and look you in the eye. Fish vision is sharp, try and wink your eyes and watch startled snappers gape their mouth, showing you their teeth, while sweetlips raise their gill and dorsal fins.

In order to experience this, remember to wear gloves so that you can hold safely to the boulders without being stung by small sea urchins or corals. Other attractions within these swim throughs and small caves are albino Neptune's cup.

Swimming away from the rocky seabed, bypassing a patch of coarse sandy area and you are within view of three underwater rock pinnacles. Circling around these unusual rock formations is great fun as you will discover shoals of pelagic fish roaming at mid waters looking for a feed on smaller fish. If you remain stationary at the bottom of the seabed and breath slowly, you may sight reef sharks. Sometimes, this dive site is also known as *Shark Site*, as divers see more sharks here than other dive sites in this region. Ocasionally, you can sight a veteran green turtle which has three legs, losing one of its legs probably to fishing nets.

This dive site offers a variety of interesting marine life, however, during low tide, the visibility can be impaired to 8 metres. Diving at peak tide should render better visibility.

Above: The titan trigger can be notorious and "attack" divers when guarding its brood.

White Rock

Located about half way between the north western coast of *Koh Tao* and *Koh Nang Yuan*, it takes about 15 minutes by boat from the pier on *Mae Haad Beach* at *Koh Tao.*

The attractions of this dive site are two submerged rock outcrops which broaden its base to form the reef bed and are homes to a wealth of marine life.

There is a prevailing current in this channel and the moving waters are constantly attracting many species of fish to feed on plankton. The presence of these plankton feeders attract predator fish, thus creating an active scenario for divers to see.

Characteristics

The tip of the rocks are just about two metres to the surface and drops to variable depths of 18 to 22 metres. Colonies of staghorn corals are apparent and they attract breams and damsels to make their homes. Formations of pore boulder corals are studded with embedded bivalves, green star corals, sea whips, orangy branching sea fans and colourful sponges form this aquatic garden.

Dive Scenes

Groupers, John snappers, smaller blue striped snappers, grey sweetlips and moray eels are sighted distinctly amongst other smaller species of resident fish. Black banded sea snakes are occasionally seen. Spinefoot fish and surgeons swim in small shoals feed nearer to the coral formations, while small yellow tails and damsels cloud mid water, often victims to garfish, barracudas, jacks and queenfish.

One of the attractions divers come to see at White Rock is a rebel titan trigger fish which have in record, made bold attacks on divers. These fish are territorial by nature, but injuring divers are only occasional when divers get too close to its lairs which may have a brood of its fry. This trigger makes diving of White Rock adventurous. You can contact Koh Tao Divers for more information, as their team have been attacked on different occasions by this fish. A diver was nipped, another received two stitches on the head and the third diver was knocked out cold.

A CHIT-CHAT ON MARINE LIFE

The alluring charms of the marine world are what divers wish to learn and they are brought to light through the pleasures of scuba diving and skin diving. Scuba diving enables man to breathe underwater with more time to discover splendours of the aquatic world. And although skin diving, limit us to a few minutes of air per dive, its silent approach, however, reveals some interesting corners of marine life which are sensitive to the sound of air bubbles.

▲ *A male cuttlefish prostrate and guards its mate while she lays eggs.*

DID YOU KNOW THAT: THE CUTTLEFISH

Cuttlefish sometimes do lay eggs on the mesh of fish traps. ➤

Cuttlefish when encountered, reveals its camouflaging skills and is a master of disguise. You are able to establish relationship with it, through careful approach and a constant subtle eye contact. All marine creatures, the fish and especially the cuttlefish are alert to the reaction of our eyes when we see them through the mask. If you glare at them, they tend to feel threatened and may flee. But when you squint your eyes smaller or give them side glances, they will be less wary.

Establishing a Relationship
When you sight a pair of cuttlefish while snorkelling, follow it with slow

Above: Extended tentacles of blue polyps feeding on adult mirco marine food.

Its colours will also change and at the end of this remarkable transformation, you can hardly notice the cuttlefish amongst the corals. At this point when you lie horizontally near it and hold your breath, you may be able to touch it by inching your fingers slowly. If it moves away a little, stop your finger movements and allow it to settle down before attempting again. When you succeed in touching it without scaring it away, you would have experienced a joy of being able to establish a relationship with the cuttlefish. *"I felt a deep sense of happiness when I had my first relationship with the cuttlefish"*.

You may sometimes see cuttlefish, amongst coral heads moving to and fro from a coral or rock crevice. Its continual display of placing its head and tentacles inside the crevice for a few seconds and withdrawing, had me puzzled when I saw this stance on two occasions while I was skin diving. My guess was that it may be laying eggs, feeding or having a game with its mate hiding in the crevice. All these "maybes" eventually zeroed in on it laying eggs, when, on my third similar encounter a soft transparent egg escaped from the crevice. It floated away with the current and as I touched it, it was so soft that I could not feel it at all. Hence this explained why I did not know it was laying eggs when I gently slipped my fingers into the crevice on both of the earlier occasions.

Another experience with the cuttlefish in a triangle affair brought greater joy when I was scuba diving off Koh Ta Chai in the Andaman Sea. A female cuttlefish was laying eggs watched over by its mate and another male intruder came along to disrupt this call of nature. The intruder was kept at bay by the

fin strokes until it decides to remain stationary in mid waters. While skindiving, take a good gulp of air and dive cautiously to about one metre from it. If it has not been threatened before, it will droop its tentacles, change its pigment to a darker tone and slowly sink to the bottom of the seabed to take refuge amongst the corals. Surface for air and do a second dive to continue observation.

When it has settled down to the bottom, approach it slowly again and stay a metre away and you will see another change. Its whole body will start to grow *"warts"* or raised cells under its skin known as *papillae* in variable sizes; until its whole body is identical to the surrounding structures.

male cuttlefish and both males displayed exceptional colours changes with raised tentacles. It was an amazing underwater scenario ever witnessed and was fortunately recorded on video and still camera. The psychedelic colours and vertical lines on the males were amazing and the wavy movements of its pectoral fins were so refined.

The female had dull colours, its tentacles drooping and its eyes half closed it was tired in this laying eggs process. During the affair, I was able to coax the male cuttlefish to rest on my palm when I removed the glove from my hand. It was a great experience and having a dive buddy to share this encounter was a greater thrill. We surfaced when our air supply was exceptionally low, but the triangle affair continued.

When you are scuba diving, you have to be more cautious if the cuttlefish is disturbed by the release of air bubbles. But the advantage of air tanks will enable you to adjust to the required situation for a relationship with the cuttlefish. Do not feel disappointed if it swims away, for it may have been frightened by divers previously. Wait for the next encounter. The best time to see the cuttlesfish in action is from late *November* to *February* in the Andaman Sea. (Refer to photo for this triangle cuttlefish affair).

THE OCTOPUS

This eight arm creature offers equally exciting moments and is not as timid as its cousin the cuttlefish. With its flexible tentacles which form three quarters of its anatomy, it is swifter in camouflaging itself when threatened.

Above: Octopus in hiding.

After witnessing its transformation, you can swim close to it slowly, because instinctly it feels that you cannot see it. If you keep a metre away and remain stationary for a few minutes, the creature will feel less threatened, relaxed its tentacles and reveal its natural self.

You may be able to coax it to feed from your hand at this stage by approaching it with a piece of fish meat. Offer a small piece of bait initially and drop it near its tentacles for it to eat freely. If it accepts the fish meat you can hold the second bait in your hand and offer it. It may reject hand feeding initially and all this depends on the

141

behaviour pattern, but your chances of success is greater than other cephalopods.

TRIGGER FISH "ATTACK"

The titan trigger fish display one of the most protective behaviour over its brood of fry when divers approach. When this fish darts in zig zag manner around you, be careful, as it may perform a *kamikaze* attack and nip you. It has a small mouth with strong top and bottom incisors which can inflict wounds, even through a wet suit.

If you encounter this aggressive behaviour swim away from that place and it will ease its attack after you are at a safe distance away. *"A rebel titan trigger fish at the White Rock dive site off Koh Tao in the Gulf of Thailand is very notorious, according to some dive operators."*

LOBSTERS

After moulting the lobsters retreat to its lairs to recuperate and wait for nature to harden its soft shell. It leaves its old shell at the entrance and divers upon sighting it will initially display some excitement. And when they pick it up I am sure a few questions will whiz through their minds.

Just a short snip story on lobster: engaged in battle over territorial rights, lobsters may lose a portion of its antennas or when overzealous divers try and grab it. However, all fractured or severed limbs will be replaced by perfect ones after moulting. They transmit a buzzing sound when threatened or when you hold them by the feelers. It searches for food buried in the seabed by using its forefront legs to feel. One of its favourite foods

are small mussels which it can break easily with its strong mandibles. The lobsters digestive system is found in its head hence it has only a head and tail.

Above: An eagle ray takes "flight".

WHEN RAYFISH "FLIES"

Ray fish do leap out of the sea and crashed with a tremendous impact when its flat body hits the waters. Why does it perform this *"flight"* in the air ? Fishermen believe that it is aborting its young, but marine experts say that it getting rid of parasites on its bodies. A manta ray repeatedly *'fly'* close to surfaced divers in the Philippines has caused me to believe that it was warding off the divers. Whatever the reasons are, the possibility of recording its action related to the birth of the young and its instinct to chase away intruders are open challenges.

CRAB STORY

On full moon nights, crabs refrain from feeding and have the instinct to mate. They lose their weight and have less meat in their bodies. Hence, when you have them as a dish during this period the meat will not be intact. Ask the fishermen and crab traders about this story.

VISIONS AND COLOURS

In the waters, things that we see through the mask appear 30 percent larger than its actual size. Corals and rocky structures may not appear startling, but marine creatures do, especially fish. The distance which a fish is sighted appears to be 25 percent nearer. In other words, the distance focused is 75 percent of the real distance. With these two optical illusions the sighting of fish, especially a shark, its size are often dramatized if a diver does not take into account these illusions.

Of changing colours in the kingdom of the living sea, their kaleidoscopic combination outshines landscape's environment. But their colour retention is controlled by the depths of the sea, which act as a natural filter that absorbs different colours at variable depths.

For example red disappears normally after 6 metres orange at approximately 12 metres and yellow in depths more than 30 metres. But these colours in the reef bounce back when a camera or video flashlight is shone on. This effect accounts for colourful underwater pictures taken in deep waters. The faint shades of blue dominate after depths of more than 30 metres.

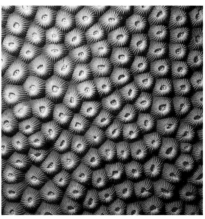

Above: Close-up view of star coral with flashlight. Found in large boulder colonies.

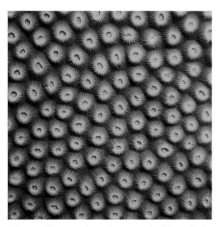

Above: Close-up view of star coral without flashlight. Found in large boulder colonies.

INFORMATION

INITIAL FIRST AID

Some knowledge of initial first aid to relieve patient of pain till medical help arrive is an advantage out in the sea. We are injured by marine creatures more often through ignorance or carelessness on our part.

Above: Lion fish shy but deadly to touch.

Venomous marine life do not attack intentionally, it is either provoked to defend itself or we accidentally come in contact with it.

Some common venomous fish: stingray, catfish, stone fish, lion and zebra fish.

Stingray and catfish are bottom feeders and the only way divers get hurt is by accidentally stepping on it. However, it is a very slim chance for this to happen even during night dives because these fish are alert species.

First Aid Suggestions
Remove victim from the sea and give an initial double dose of pain relieving tablets with warm water. Expose afflicted area if under wet suit or remove gently the fins or dive boots if the foot is injured.

Lie the victim down, raise the injured limb and rinse the wound with antiseptic wash and apply bearable warm water to soften the skin for easy removal of spines. Apply pressure and bleed the wound and continue soaking the afflicted area in warm water for a few minutes and this will relief much of the pain. Apply antiseptic cream and keep the wound clean for further medical treatment.

Stone fish inflict intense pain and the venom is more poisonous. Fortunately this fish is not common. Their characteristics of being dormant and well camouflaged and will hardly move even if you are very close, give reasons to be more wary when touching rocky seabeds. Divers fall victim when they are not careful when it is necessary to hold onto undulating seabed while working against current or attending to other matters.

Lion/zebra fish belongs to the scorpion fish family. Its feather-like fins are graceful but have venomous stings. It is unlikely for divers to be stung by this fish unless they attempt to catch with their hands or touch it when it is cornered in a dead end crevice. Their movements are slow and graceful and will normally swim away when divers swim too close.

First Aid Suggestions
Victims of both these fish will experience excruciating pain and swelling in the wound. Apply the same first aid treatment as for stingray. The spines may be more difficult to remove being finer. Reassure the victim and apply soft solution of potassium permanganate while awaiting for proper medical treatment.

Other venomous marine creatures: jellyfish, stinging hydroids, sea urchins, fire corals and cone shells.

Jellyfish are always subject to the flow of current or moves very sluggishly close to the surface. Hence, contact with them is made when divers are not careful when descending or ascending and get into their way.

Sea urchins are bottom dwellers and juveniles are found amongst nooks and crannies of rock boulders. Beginners to scuba diving when they have not learned the art of neutral buoyancy are likely to be hurt by sea urchins on the seabed. Accidents through careless holding of rocky surfaces where young sea urchins are embedded is common among inexperienced divers.

Above: Sea urchin.

Their spines are very brittle and breaks easily in the skin. The removing of these spines are difficult due to the multiple fine barbs on the spines

Stinging Hydroids are strange looking animals in colonies that looks like feathery ferns in the water. They belie their stinging characteristics and unwary divers come in contact feel a sudden stinging sensation. Divers once stung will be twice shy and stay alert during dives.

Fire corals got its name for their painful stings it inflicts when divers accidentally brush their skin against it. They grow with other hard corals on the reef and look very ordinary, with stubby branches like juvenile moose antler corals. They appear yellowish brown with pale white tint on their tips.

145

Above: Stinging feathery hydroids.

First Aid Suggestions:
For *jellyfish, sea urchins, stinging hydroids* and *fire corals,* lie the victim down and speak with reassuring words. Use some diluted vinegar to pour on the affected area. Apply anti-inflammation cream on the affected area and if patient is in pain, administer pain relieving tablets before seeking medical attention.

Above: Fire coral.

If it is *jellyfish* sting and the tentacles are still on the victim, remove them gently with glove or wet sand if available. Do not try rubbing off the tentacles as it will cause the cells to fire the stings.

When *sea urchin's* spines are embedded in the skin, apply methylated spirit and warm water which will ease the pain and soften the skin. This will make removal of spines easier, although the barbed spines are difficult to remove. If the remaining spines are small pieces, near the skin surface, you may hit the affected area with a firm object like the metal base of some heavy diving knife handle. This will cause the spines to further break into smaller pieces and be absorbed by the tissues. Seek medical help if the spines are embedded deep. Apply antiseptic cream before proper medical attention is available to prevent infection.

Dangerous cone shells: Some cone shells are venomous and possesses harpoon like stings which are capable of puncturing thin dive suits, bags or gloves. Certain species are highly dangerous and can be fatal. Victim suffers severe pain, numbness, nausea and foaming from the mouth and in serious cases, blurring of vision, lost of muscular reflexes and respiratory problems. The most dangerous cone shell is the *Conus geographus* which is known to have caused several death is also found in Thailand waters.

First Aid Suggestions:
Keep victim calm in a lying position. Wash affected area with antiseptic solution, apply bearable warm water to reduce pain and soften the skin for easier removal of harpoon. After removing, bleed the wound and apply antiseptic solution and cream.

146

Administer pain relieving tablets and seek medical help as soon as possible.

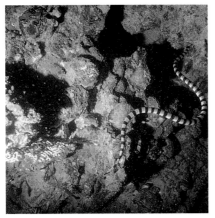

Above: Sea snake.

Prevention is better than treatment, so do be alert and be wary of which are the dangerous marine creatures. Remember, marine creatures are not aggressive by nature and we should not be afraid of them, but respect and appreciate their beauty as a guest in their underwater world.

Nitrogen Narcosis and Decompression Sickness
These two after-dive *unpleasant effects* are shunned by all divers and if it does happen, if you should go diving in Thailand, the following information will be most useful.

Bangkok Metropolitan Area:
Division of Underwater and Aviation Medicine
Department of Medicine,
Royal Thai Navy
Taksin Road, Thonburi
Bangkok 10600
Tel: 4601105
(Office Hours: 0830–1630 hours)

(Emergency Service: 24 hours)
Chamber Type: Multiplace double locks Hyperbaric Chamber — 12 persons.

Eastern Region:
Sections of Underwater and Aviation Medicine
Division of Internal Medicine
Apakorn Kiatiwong Hospital
Sattahip Naval Base
Sattahip, Chonburi
Tel: (038) 436164
(Office hours: 0830–1630 hours)
(Emergency Service: 24 hours)
Chamber Type: Multiplace double locks Hyperbaric Chamber — 6 persons.

Above: Exposed — the golden lips of a thorny oyster.

DIVE SUITS — ITS IMPORTANCE AND FASHION

Although the Andaman Sea and the Gulf of Thailand waters are relatively warm, it is recommended that you wear an appropriate dive suit for an enjoyable dive.

The plankton rich waters not only keeps the population of fish life prolific,

147

it also maintains healthy communities of coral reefs and shells. During certain times of the seasons, they reproduce by releasing eggs and sperms in external fertilization. The results will be millions of spore swimming in the waters. These tiny animals cause minor irritations on the skin which will disrupt your joy of diving or snorkeling if you are not wearing a dive suit.

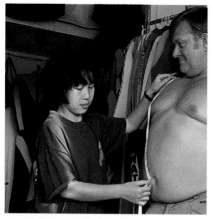

Above: Custom made dive suits give divers greater comfort and joy in scuba diving — Phuket Wet Suit.

In the water, the body heat is absorbed 25 times faster than air and adding to the fact that sometimes there are cold currents, diving can be a shivering experience without a wet suit.

Engrossed with the spectacles of coral gardens and exotic fish life, we sometimes accidentally brush against live corals and stinging hydroids that cause nasty abrasions and stings. A wet suit or a dive suit will prevents these unpleasantness.

Wet suits offer thermal protection from cold and also increase positive buoyancy. Extra weights must be added on to your weight belt to assist in descending. If you are accustom totemperate waters, a thin lycra dive suit will be enough and you need not add on the extra weights.

Not all dive shops have wet suits or dive suits for rent and those which have them may not have your size. Divers in Thailand can now have their wet or dive suit custom made in Phuket and Pattaya. There are currently a shop at each of these two dive destinations

A silhouette of bat fish in mid waters.

148

which stocks multi-coloured quality imported materials.

Above: Symbosis harmony.

Dive fashion is the trend in this sport and you can have your favourite colour combination with extra features like hood, pockets, elbow and knee pads and your personal name or logo sewn on too. Custom made suits make you feel comfortable and look smart on the boat and in the waters.

You can have your personal wet suit or lycra dive suit made within 48 hours at:

Phuket Wetsuits and Sporting Fashions
25/5 Moo 9, Chaofa Road
Phuket 83130
Tel: (076) 381818 Fax: (076) 381260
Sea and Oilfield Services Co Ltd
1/1 Moo 3, Pattaya-Naklua Road
Chonburi 20150
Tel: (038) 221860-1 Fax: (038) 221618

"A Wet Suit's Voice"
Most divers have difficulties when slipping their feet and hands through tight fitting wet suits. The effort can be strenuous, especially when you are dressing up on a wobbling longtail boat.

Try this method: wear a plastic bag on your hands or feet when you are slip-ping on the wet suit and your limbs will slide through the openings smoothly.

DIVE TERMS

Dive	Dam nam
Fin	Tin pet
Mask	Na kak
Regulator	Regulator
Snorkel	Tor hai chai
B.C.	B.C.
Weight	Nam nak
Tank	Tank
Torchlight	Fai chai
Follow	Tarm
Current	Kak sae nam
Fast	Reo
Slow	Cha
Danger	Anta-rai
Careful	Lakmat lawang
Water	Nam
High tide	Nam kherng
Low tide	Nam long
Big waves	Khluen yai
Strong wind	Lom raeng
Fine weather	Akat dee
Hot Weather	Akat rawn
Rain	Fon-tok
Sun burn	Daet phao
North	Nua
South	Tai
East	Tawanork
West	Tawan tok
Deep	Luk
Shallow	Tern
Sand	Sai
Boat	Reua
Hire boat	Chao reua
How much	Thao rai
Per day	Neun wan
Per hour	Neun shua-mong
Cave	Tham
Coral	Pakarang
Shell	Hoi
Fish	Pla

Crab	*Poo*
Squid	*Pla muk*
Octopus	*Pla muk yak*
Lobster	*Kung mangkorn*
Turtle	*Tao*
Shark	*Pla chalam*
Whale Shark	*Pla chalam wan*
Stingray	*Pla karben*
Grouper	*Pla kow*
Sweetlip	*Pla moo*
Trevally	*Pla mong*
Jack	*Pla mong*
Snapper	*Pla kapong*
Queen fish	*Pla siak*
Bream	*Pla tamak*
Mullet	*Pla kabok*
Barracuda	*Pla sak*
Tuna	*Pla O*
Mackerel	*Pla insee*
Dolphin	*Pla loma*
Garfish	*Pla toong*
Sole fish	*Pla lin-fai*
Rabbit fish	*Pla kitang*
Surgeon fish	*Pla kitang*
Goby	*Pla boo*
Parrot fish	*Pla nok kaeo*
Butterfly fish	*Pla phee seua*
Clown fish	*Pla katoon*

Above: Sea Gypsies on Surin Island at Chong Kad Beach.

TIPS ON THAI WAYS

An exchange of culture shocks is sometimes inevitable when the west meets the east, but when you are learning to respect and understand the Thai culture and customs, your holiday in Thailand will be more enjoyable.

"Wai" is a gesture of greeting where both hands join together as in prayer at face level, with the head slightly bowing to superiors or equal social status. When returning a *"wai"* to someone junior, the *"wai"* is held at chest level with a smile. It is a very respectful apology gesture that has resolved many a social upheaval.

When you are greeting a Thai with a *"wai"*, say *"Sawadee"*, which means a string of nice words like, "welcome", "hello", "greetings". If you unintentionally offend someone, the *"wai"* action followed by the word *"khor thot"* which means "sorry" will be accepted as a sincere apology.

It is a social demerit to lose one's temper or to show appall in a problem situation. A practice of tolerance, patience and a soft tone of voice are adopted by the Thais in overcoming a misunderstanding.

All Buddhist images in temples, caves or any religious sites must be treated with respect. Dress modestly when visiting these places and remember to take off your foot wear when entering a temple. Ladies are prohibited to touch or brush against the robe of a monk. Offerings to be given to him should preferably be conducted by a man, or placed it the alm bowl which the monk carries.

Affection in the public is considered a bad taste, so are topless appearance on the beach. Thailand is a Buddhist nation and the law is very tolerant, but if you are outraged, the law will come to your assistance and later may punish you too.

The head is the noblest part of the body and should not be touched. Patting someone on the head or hair ruffling may seem harmless in some countries, but taboo in Thailand. The feet is considered the lowest part of your body and thus when you are sitting, do not point it at anyone sitting opposite you, it is more apparent when sitting on the floor.

The Royal Families are greatly respected and nobody in exception can be tolerated for showing any form of disrespect. If a Thai coin should fall, do not attempt to step it with your feet. Allow it to stop naturally as it bears the King's picture.

The word *"khun"* is the proper way to address both man and woman, followed by their first name. For example, if your name is John Smith, the Thai will call you Khun John.

Be mindful of these few tips and your stay will draw no frowns but more smiles for happier moments of your holiday.

A cluster of yellow "sun-corals".

TOURISM AUTHORITY OF THAILAND (TAT)
(LOCAL AND OVERSEAS OFFICE)

Head Office:
Ratchadamnoen Nok Avenue, Bangkok 10100, THAILAND. Tel: 282-1143, 282-4175 Cable: TOT BANGKOK Telex: 84194 TATBKK TH Fax: 66 2 280-1744.

Local Offices
PHUKET
73-75 Phuket Road, Amphoe Muang, Phuket 83000 Tel: (076) 212-213, 211-036 Fax: 66 076 213-582

SURAT THANI
5 Talat Mai Road, Ban Don, Amphoe Muang, Surat Thani 84000 Tel: (077) 282-828, 281-828, Fax: 66 077 282-828.

Overseas Offices:
ASIA & PACIFIC
HONG KONG:
Room 401 Fairmont House, 8 Cotton Tree Drive, Central, HONG KONG Tel: 868-0732, 868-0854
Cable: HK THAITOUR Telex: 63092 HKTAT HX Fax: 868-4585
Area of Responsibility: Hong Kong, Taiwan, Macau and People's Republic of China

KUALA LUMPUR:
C/O Royal Thai Embassy, 206 Jalan Ampang, Kuala Lumpur, MALAYSIA.
Tel: (093) 248-0958 Telex: 31089 TATKL MA Fax: (093) 241-3002
Area of Responsibility: Malaysia and Brunei Darussalam

OSAKA:
Hiranomachi Yachiyo Bldg. 5F., 1-8-13 Hiranomachi Chuo-ku Osaka 541, JAPAN.
Tel: (06) 231-4434 Telex: 64675 TATOSAKA J Fax: (06) 231-4337
Area of Responsibility: Southern Japan

TOKYO:
Hibiya Mitsui Bldg., 1-2 Yurakucho 1-Chome, Chiyoda-ku, Tokyo 100, JAPAN,
Tel: (03) 580-6776-7, 508-0237 Cable: THAITOUR TOKYO Telex: 33946
TATTOKYO J Fax: 03-508-7808
Area of Responsibility: Northern Japan, Korea

SINGAPORE
C/O Royal Thai Embassy, 370 Orchard Road, Singapore 0923, SINGAPORE.
Tel: (65) 235-7694, 235-7901, Cable: THAITOUR SINGAPORE Telex: 39428 TATSIN RS
Fax: 733-5653
Area of Responsibility: Singapore, Indonesia and Philippines.

SYDNEY:
12th Floor, Royal Exchange Bldg. 56 Pitt Street, Sydney 2000, AUSTRALIA.
Tel: (02) 247-7549, 247-7540 Cable: THAITOUR SYDNEY Telex: 23467 THAITC AA
Fax: (02) 251-2465
Area of Responsibility: Australia, New Zealand and South Pacific

EUROPE
FRANKFURT:
Thailändisches Fremdenverkehrsbüro, BethmannStr. 58/IV D-6000 Frankfurt/M.I., WEST
GERMANY. Tel: (069) 295-704, 295-804 Cable: THAITOUR Frankfurt/M. Telex: 413542
TAFRA D Fax: (069) 281-468
Area of Responsibility: East Europe and Switzerland

LONDON:
49 Albemarle Street, London WIX 3 FE, England U.K. Tel: (01) 499-7679
Cable: THAITOUR LONDON Telex: 24136 TATLON G Fax (01) 629-5519
Area of Responsibility: United Kingdom, North Ireland, Iceland, Finland and Scandinavia

PARIS:
Office National du Tourisme de Thilande, 90 Avenue des Champs Elysées, 75008 Paris, FRANCE. Tel: 4562-8656, 4562-8748 Cable: THAITOUR PARIS Telex: 650093 TATPAR F Fax: (01) 4563-7888
Area of Responsibility: France, Belgium, Luxembourg, the Netherlands

ROME:
Ente Nazionale per il Turismo Thailandese Via Barberini, 50 00187 Roma, ITALY. Tel: (06) 474-7410, 474-7660 Telex: 626139 TAT I Fax: (06) 474-7660
Area of Responsibility: Italy, Spain, Greece, Portugal, Israel, Egypt, Turkey

NORTH AMERICA
NEW YORK:
5 World Trade Centre, Suite No. 2449, New York, N.Y. 10048, U.S.A. Tel: (212) 432-0433-35 Cable: THAITOUR NEW YORK Telex: 667612 TOT UW Fax: 212 912-0920
Area of Responsibility: Eastern U.S.A. and Eastern Canada

LOS ANGELES:
3440 Wilshire Blvd., Suite 1101, Los Angeles, CA 90010, U.S.A. Tel: (213) 382-2353-55 Cable: THAITOUR LOS ANGELES Telex: 686208 TTC LSA Fax: 213 380-6476.
Area of Responsibility: Western U.S.A., Latin America, Western Canada

A Salute To all Conservation Divers.
Sharing the *"treasures"* of the living sea is our pride and joy.

Tourism Authority of Thailand

The Ascend.

INDEX